Direct Mail Pal

Direct Mail Pal
A Direct Mail Production Handbook

By

T.J. Tedesco
Ken Boone
Terry Woods
John Leonard

GATFPress
PITTSBURGH

International Standard Book Number: 0-88362-378-1
Library of Congress Catalog Card Number: 2002102478

Printed in the United States of America
Catalog No. 1727
First Edition, Second Printing, February 2003

Printed on Williamsburg Offset, 60-lb., smooth finish by
International Paper

GATFPress books are widely used by companies, associations, and
schools for training, marketing, and resale. Quantity discounts are
available by contacting Peter Oresick at 800/910-GATF.

GATF*Press*

Graphic Arts Technical Foundation
200 Deer Run Road
Sewickley, PA 15143-2600
Phone: 412/741-6860
Fax: 412/741-2311
Internet: www.gain.net

Printing Industries of America
100 Daingerfield Road
Alexandria, VA 22314-2888
Phone: 703/519-8100
Fax: 703/548-3227
Internet: www.gain.net

Orders to:
GATF Orders
P.O. Box 1020
Sewickley, PA 15143-1020
Phone (U.S.): 800/662-3916 • Phone (Canada): 613/236-7208
Phone (all other countries): 412/741-5733
Fax: 412/741-0609 • Online: www.gain.net

Contents

Section 3—Direct Mail Production

Section 4—Direct Mail Post-Production

Appendices

Glossaries

Index 259

About the Authors 266

About GATF 269

About PIA 270

GATF*Press:* Selected Titles..271

Colophon...272

Preface

A few weeks before the manuscript for this book was submitted to our publisher, the awful events of September 11, 2001, occurred. We briefly considered rewriting portions of *Direct Mail Pal* to discuss more security issues, but decided against this course of action for two primary reasons:

1. Good direct mail services production companies have always emphasized security in their plants. These are "behind-the-scenes" issues and should remain that way.

2. Although evil people can usually find a way to do harm in creative ways, the United States Postal Service (USPS) and Canadian Postal Corporation (CPC) remain the best mail delivery systems in the world. We should let the USPS and the CPC deliver the mail while we focus on generating profits through well-designed and well-implemented direct mail programs.

Let there be no doubt: We are a resilient people living in the finest part of the world. The way Americans and Canadians conduct business will change only on our terms, when we wish.

Acknowledgments

This book wouldn't have been possible without contributions from many people and organizations. Special thanks go to:

• **Mark Beard**, president, Finishbinders, Inc., 1900 Delaware Ave., Des Moines, IA 50317, for his help with chapter 38. He can be reached at 888-788-7314 or mark@finishbinders.com.

• **Sylvia Konkel**, vice president, marketing, EU Services, 649 N. Horners Lane, Rockville, MD 20850, for her help on chapter 24. She can be reached at 800-230-3362 or SKonkel@euservices.com.

• **Jack Rickard**, president, Rickard Bindery, 325 N. Ashland Avenue, Chicago, IL 60607-1001, for his help with chapters 3, 33, 34, and 35. He can be reached at 800-747-1389 or jack@rickardbindery.com.

• **Frank Shear**, president, Seaboard Bindery, 10 Linscott Road, Woburn, MA 01801, for his help with chapter 9. He can be reached at 781-932-3908 or frank@seaboardbindery.com.

• **Art Simpson**, executive vice president, EU Services, 649 N. Horners Lane, Rockville, MD 20850, for his help on chapter 22. He can be reached at 800-230-3362 or ASimpson@euservices.com.

• **Brenda Slacum**, chief operating officer, Specialties Bindery, 4815 Lawrence Street, Hyattsville, MD 20781, for her help with chapter 33. Brenda can be reached at 800-638-5667, or brenda@specialtiesbindery.com.

• **Adam Van Wye**, vice president, Mailing Lists, Inc., 10916 Outpost Drive, Gaithersburg, MD 20878, for his help with chapter 16. He can be reached at (800) 570-LIST (5478) or mailvan@aol.com.

• **Blaine Haverty,** director of marketing, Sure-Feed Engineering, Inc., 3360 Scherer Drive, St. Petersburg, FL 33716, for providing photographs of the FlowMaster 12000 inserter. He can be reached at 800-INSERTER or bhaverty@ sure-feed.com

In addition, appreciation needs to be extended to several publishing companies and individual publications for all their guidance, patience, and support throughout the years. These are:

• *DM News* is a leading publication serving the direct mail industry and is located at 100 Avenue of the Americas, New York, NY 10013, 212-925-7300. Thanks goes to **Scott Hovanyetz,** associate editor, and **Tad Clark,** editor.

• **Cygnus Business Media, Inc.,** publishes *Print and Graphics, Printing Views, Southern Graphics, Printing Journal, Quick Printing,* and *Printing News.* Cygnus Business Media, Inc. is located at 445 Broad Hollow Road, Melville, NY 11747-4722, 800-447-4237. Special thanks go to **David Lindsay,** editor in chief.

• **Innes Publishing Co.** publishes *High Volume Printing, Instant & Small Commercial Printer, In-Plant Printer,* and *The Binding Edge.* Innes Publishing Co. can be reached at P.O. Box 7280, Libertyville, IL 60048, 847-816-7900. Special thanks go to **Ray Roth,** editor in chief, and **Mary Ellin Innes,** president.

• *Printing Impressions* is a leading publication serving the printing industry and is located at 401 N. Broad Street, Philadelphia, PA 19108, 215-238-5300. Special thanks goes to **Mark T. Michelson,** editor in chief.

• *American Printer* is a leading publication serving the printing industry and is located at 29 N. Wacker Drive, Chicago, IL 60607, 312-726-2802. Thanks go to **Katherine O'Brien,** editorial director.

• *Graphic Arts Monthly* is a leading publication serving the printing industry and is located at 345 Hudson Street, New York, NY 10014, 212-519-7326. Thanks go to **Roger Ynostroza,** editor in chief.

• *Advents* is a leading direct mail publication serving the Mid-Atlantic direct mail community and can be reached at 7702 Leesburg Pike, Tyson's Corner, VA 22043-2612, 703-590-9996. Special thanks go to **Nancy Scott,** editor.

Other contributors include Bill Alpert, Marty Anson, Eric Bauer, Lorraine Beard, Erik Bohnenstengel, Rick Carletti, Dave Clossey, Randy Doman, David Dunnett, Marty Duran, Jim Egan, Jim Freisinger, John Goché, Russ Haines, Sue Hein, Barry Heyman, Brian Hills, Kurt Hoffman, Bob Janes, Gary Junge, Mike Keenan, Mark Lee, John Mackey, Bill Main, T.J. Manning, Gary Markovits, Robert Mason, Matthew McBride, Gary McCants, Pete Perlo, Peggy Rhoades, Kevin Rickard, Tom Ross, Rod Rothermel, Frank Shear, Harold Shear, Jim Shear, Charlie Smith, Christopher Tessier, Bob Tier, Bill Ulrich, Bob Windler, and Kathi Young.

Introduction

Direct Mail Pal: A Direct Mail Production Handbook takes readers through a comprehensive exploration of the world of direct mail. Against the backdrop of more promotional options than ever before, we present the ongoing benefits of direct mail in a positive, but realistic, light.

Direct Mail Pal is comprised of five main sections:

- Direct Mail Today—Common direct mail concepts and products
- Direct Mail Pre-Production—Project planning, layouts, and front end data concepts
- Direct Mail Production—Data management, imaging, lettershop, and bindery operations
- Direct Mail Post-Production—Improving future performance by analyzing past performance
- Appendices—Practical direct mail nuts and bolts information for everyday use

The first section covers important general business concepts, including account management, communication, and quality assurance. Effective marketing depends on using the best available promotional tools to influence buying behavior. None of the big four promotional categories—direct sales, airwave media, direct mail/printing, and e-commerce/Internet—are going to disappear anytime soon. Media convergence is a good thing, even for those in the direct mail industry. As many dot-com companies have discovered, the inherent promotional weakness of the e-world means that the demand for promotional printed materials such as direct mail will increase in the foreseeable future.

In sections two through four, we get to the heart of direct mail planning, production, and analysis. The topics discussed are pertinent for most entry- and mid-level professionals.

The appendices deserve careful review. This is where you'll find useful operating tips, procedures, and management forms. Put this section to work for your organization.

*   *   *

The target audience for *Direct Mail Pal* can be divided into two main categories:

1. Printing and direct mail customer service and sales professionals, estimators, production managers, and lettershop and bindery employees

Growth-oriented printing and direct mail companies recognize that the training process never stops. This comprehensive book is both informational and accessible to mid- and entry-level direct mail and printing professionals. Basic direct mail knowledge is an under-represented skill set in the graphic arts industry, and those with a good command of these processes will do their jobs better. Careful study of this book will help readers advance their careers.

2. Marketers, agency employees, and graphic designers

Many marketers and graphic designers don't understand what is possible, or what is cost-effective, when planning direct mail programs. This lack of knowledge hampers their ability to serve clients and limits their professional growth. Marketers and designers will appreciate this book's down-to-earth descriptions of direct mail processes that are not overly technical.

One last point: The authors have attempted to minimize the distinction between the United States Postal Service (USPS) and the Canada Postal Corporation (CPC). It would have made for tedious reading had all references been adjusted for country differences. Readers should be able to easily distinguish when U.S. and Canadian examples are used.

SECTION 1 Direct Mail Today

Direct Mail: A Compelling Way to Spread Your Word

When American Express launched its Optima credit card, they turned to direct mail. When they needed to save its corporate card, again they relied on direct mail to carry a disproportionate share of the marketing burden. How about other financial institutions offering credit cards? General Motors also went the direct mail route when they launched the GM Visa card—the largest affinity card program ever! They too discovered that direct mail works.

The examples go on and on. The phenomenal success of the book *How to Win Friends and Influence People* by Dale Carnegie was in part due to a direct mail piece that accounted for a million books being sold in three years. When subscription rates need to be boosted, where do high-profile magazines like *Sports Illustrated, Money,* and *Time* turn? The answer is direct mail once again. How about companies like Air France, Apple Computer, Blockbuster Video, Colgate-Palmolive, Sony, Nintendo, or even the U.S. Army? They all rely on direct mail for one reason: It works.

According to a 1999 study by the Printing Industries of America's Graphic Arts Marketing Information Service (GAMIS)—*The Status and Future of Direct Mail*—the size of the U.S. advertising industry was $264 billion in 1998. Of that amount, $29 billion or 11%, was comprised of direct mail expenditures. In addition, Canada adds another $1.5 billion to the North American total. GAMIS forecasts that the size of the total direct mail market will increase at an average of 6% per year in 1999 dollars.

Why does this seemingly old-fashioned method of contacting customers and prospects have such an attractive future? Unlike broadcast and print advertising media that does not elicit a direct response, direct mail is accountable. Every cent involved in producing a direct mail campaign is easily tallied, and each response can be tracked. Future decisions can be made based on past results. Combining today's abundant wealth of consumer data with sophisticated imaging technology makes true one-to-one direct response marketing a reality.

It's a testament to our industry when an advertising legend such as David Olgivy, founder of the high-profile advertising agency Olgivy & Mather, claims that direct mail was his first love and secret weapon.

> I have been a voice crying in the wilderness, trying to persuade the advertising establishment to take direct mail more seriously and to stop treating its practitioners as non-commissioned officers. It was my secret weapon in the avalanche of new business acquisitions that made Olgivy & Mather an instant success. (David Olgivy, 1983)

PAL POINT... No matter your involvement in the advertising and promotional industries, do right by your customers by being a strong direct mail advocate. Make sound business decisions by correctly assessing your promotional and informational needs, choosing the right direct mail options, and then evaluating your results. In short, learn your craft well so you can be a valuable resource to your company and customers.

A Brief History of Direct Mail

In some respects, mailing is an extension of the graphic arts industry. Like printers and trade binderies, direct mailing services companies enhance the value of paper by changing its form. The direct mail industry is constantly evolving, and today it's vastly different than it was as recently as twenty years ago.

Let's start by saying that direct mail marketing is the means of targeting individuals with the highest propensity to respond to a marketing or promotional message. Every production issue theoretically is in pursuit of achieving this objective. Now let's move on to various production issues.

Top-quality prepress, printing, binding, and finishing services don't make a bit of difference unless the final printed product gets into the hands of the target audience. Today, there is still no better way to quickly deliver large quantities of printed products than direct mail. To better manage the direct mail process, it's useful to understand how our seemingly complicated mailing environment came to be.

Direct Mail Processing

In the late 1960s, the computer found its way into list maintenance. At this point, the direct mail industry rapidly changed from metal plate addressing to data card addressing to computerized label generation. With computers, maintaining mailing files became significantly easier and record "selection" (targeted mailings) became feasible. Although most databases were developed and maintained by individual companies, the end product was generally four-up Cheshire labels printed in zip code order.

The United States Post Office (USPS) attempted postal cost reduction by encouraging large-volume mailers to prepare their mailings in a fashion that would minimize postal handling. In 1977, the USPS offered a discount for "carrier route presort," which reduced postage costs for mail prepared by individual carrier route. By giving mail bundles directly to mail carriers, the USPS eliminated a number of sorting steps, and costs did go down. Appending carrier route information to data files while simultaneously pursuing the postal discount qualification process caused many mailers to abandon homegrown software in favor of standard presort programs.

Throughout much of the 1980s, mail presorting was primarily done on mainframe computers with expensive software. In the 1990s, this software became widely available on PCs, and a large number of individual users were capable of preparing their own mailing files. The output of these presorting programs slowly changed from Cheshire labels to an electronic medium capable of driving high-speed inkjet and laser printers. Today, presorted files frequently have to factor in drop-ship consolidation and commingling of mail to achieve the maximum postal discounts. To give you an idea of how quickly the direct mail industry has changed, the USPS has made more changes in its last five years than in its first two hundred.

Mail Preparation

Mail preparation equipment has evolved from slow, simple machines requiring a number of operators to fast, automated one-operator ones. Today high-speed imaging devices have largely replaced Cheshire labels. While there are many imaging techniques available, the direct mail industry is dominated by laser and inkjet printing. Customers seeking high quality and large image areas generally prefer laser printing. If personalization is required on only a small portion of the printed product, i.e., name and address, inkjet printing is more attractive.

Recently, great strides have been made toward bridging the quality gap between inkjet and laser printing. Today, there are inkjet units that not only produce images as large as laser printer output (with the same font selection), but also do so faster and cheaper. The resolution standard for inkjet printing is now 240×240 dpi, while laser printing is 300×300 dpi or higher. After imaging, more online or offline postpress processes can be done, or the job can directly enter the mail stream. Generally, laser-printed forms are personalized box to box or roll to roll, then converted, folded, and glue-sealed, tab-sealed, or inserted into an envelope. A lot of time and money can be saved when inkjet imaging is done inline with other paper conversion processes.

The final step is to correctly package the mail to maximize postal discounts. Mailbags, like Cheshire labels, are all but dead. Non-letter mail palletization qualification has been reduced to a 250-lb. (113-kg) minimum, enabling mail bundling by proper qualification level. Mail bundles are placed on pallets with destination placards affixed to each pallet. Postal trays, which protect and maintain proper mail orientation, can be used for both first-class and bulk letter mail.

Backend Postal Discounting

Until 1993, a mailing job ended after USPS verification. Now, the USPS encourages more cost-saving steps, including commingling of mail and drop shipments. Commingling (pooling the mail from several companies together) reduces postage expense by creating larger zip-code strings. Commingling means that a lot of mail that previously would have traveled at basic rates is lowered to three-digit rates, while much of the three-digit mail is now charged at five-digit mail rates.

Since presort machines commingle jobs at 30,000 to 40,000 pieces per hour, large mailing companies can offer postage savings far in excess of additional processing costs. Needless to say, this is a classic win-win-win situation because customers incur less postage costs, mailers make more money, and the USPS reduces processing time. Unfortunately, presort machines are expensive and generally are found at only the largest of high-volume mailers.

The USPS allows drop shipment discounts for mail delivered directly to bulk mail centers (BMCs) and an even larger discount for mail transported directly to destination section center facilities (SCFs). Large-volume mailers are often able to consolidate several customers on one truck and return more than 50% of the increased postal discount to their clients. Smaller mailers that don't have the consistent high volume necessary to support an in-house consolidation program can use "consolidators" for this purpose. With a consolidator, small-volume mailers may still be able to return as much as 25% of the gross savings to the client.

PAL POINT... Direct mail has changed a lot. Over the years, the emphasis has drifted from mechanical efficiency to electronic wizardry. In addition, keeping abreast of the changing postal climate is more important now than ever. Investing the time to find the right mailing partner and develop a good working relationship with your postal representative will significantly benefit you...and likely save you a lot of money.

3

Convergence: Direct Mail, Electronic, Print, and Airwave Media

—with Jack Rickard, President, Rickard Bindery

Many people consider time their most valuable asset. Direct mail is a uniquely effective way to reach people because it allows consumers to gather information about goods, services, or almost anything else whenever and wherever they want. Good information is required to make educated buying decisions. To that end, direct mail is an invaluable asset. We're going to take a step back for a moment and consider all print media, including direct mail, for this chapter.

Are you concerned about the e-commerce wave? Can you remember a time when the graphic communications and advertising industries didn't feel "threatened" by one new technology or another? First, it was the telephone; then radio, television, and the "paperless society." Sure, each development affected business, but as long as those in the direct mail industry caught the wave, we were fine. Smart direct marketers aren't scared of e-commerce, instead they are just dusting off their surfboards.

Yes, direct mail and print markets are changing. Computer manuals have far fewer pages than they did five years ago. In-store product catalogs are rapidly going digital. The forms business has been hurt. According to a 2000 Raine Consulting industry study, the printed publications market will drop from $39 billion in 1999 to $29 billion by 2005. On the other hand, Raine predicts that the market for promotional printing will increase 50%, to a whopping $52 billion, over the next five years. Although the printing industry has begun to experience a slowdown in its rate of growth, few are forecasting an actual decrease.

There is sustainable growth in some direct mail markets, and our challenge is to position our own companies by making the right strategic choices. Smart marketers will take advantage of the best promotional tools available to them and select a mix of marketing vehicles that achieves their business goals. E-commerce will have a vital role to play—and so will print and its subset, direct mail.

A large percentage of commercially printed matter attempts to separate customers from their discretionary dollars. Until recently, marketers had three primary categories of promotional activities within which to engage:

- Sales—In person, telephone, or email
- Airwaves—Radio or television
- Print—Direct mail, advertising, billboards, etc.

Now, they have one more:

- E-commerce—Transactions over the Internet

Throw out the hype. As exciting as e-commerce is, it really is just another category of promotional tool in a savvy marketer's arsenal. Each category has pros and cons.

The Big Four

Sales. Sales activity is very personal and very effective. However, a sales force is an expensive proposition and is inappropriate for many types of products and services.

Airwaves. Television and radio reach a lot of people at a relatively low cost per impression. However, the Achilles heel of airwave media is that the pitch gets to the consumer on the advertiser's schedule, not the consumer's. This means that both television and radio are poorly suited for direct response because most people can't remember phone numbers, store locations, and website addresses unless they happen to have a writing or recording instrument handy. Viewers and listeners will get a basic idea about what is being pitched, but taking action is difficult. Moreover, channel surfing during commercials seems to be on the rise.

Print. Print is convenient. One of the major benefits of this category is that people can view promotional materials on their own schedule, not the advertisers'. Then, if they choose to take action, they can bring the printed piece with them for reference purposes while making telephone calls or accessing websites. Yes, some forms of print behave more like airwave media (i.e., billboards and signage), but print in general and direct mail specifically is easily stored and highly portable.

The Internet. The Internet offers improvement over both print and airwave marketing in two significant ways. First, it performs exceptionally well for executing simple transactions in a "point and click" environment. Second, it is a low-cost way to provide lots of information to the marketplace and keep it current. However, as a promotional medium, the Internet is weak. Soliciting to "opt-in" lists is generally okay, but as people get more and more fed up with email and banner advertising overload, click-through rates will plunge. Violation of electronic privacy is hardly something to be trifled with. With a few keystrokes, angry customers can literally send out millions of defamatory emails or launch spiteful websites.

Other Factors

There are other topics to consider. First, direct mail pieces can be almost any size, giving this media an unencumbered field of vision. Although electronic pages can be unlimited in size too, their practical viewing area is limited by the size of the viewer's computer monitor. Side-by-side product comparisons from different companies are easy to do if the medium is print—just spread out competing catalogs and brochures on a large, flat surface. Comparison shopping on the Web is possible, but it requires toggling prowess and effective management of limited viewing space.

Also, current pixel technology means that image reproduction on computer monitors is of lesser quality than print. For example, consider how people buy furniture. Stores, catalogs, and websites are three popular ways. As in many businesses, maintaining low return rates is critically important, and return rates are lowest when customers' expectations are met. When you buy furniture off a store floor, you're pretty sure about the quality you're going to get. When you order from an image, whether digital or printed, the product better match your expectations or you might return it. In order to attract business, furniture dot-coms offer extremely liberal return policies to convince their target audiences to try their services. This can be a dangerous way of doing business—as Living.com discovered when its return rate exceeded 40%, causing it to go out of business. The bottom line is that images must accurately depict the product, and print is still best at doing this.

What Are Smart Marketers Doing?

According to a widely accepted business school marketing model, marketers should lead their target audiences through the four AIDA steps: awareness, interest, desire, and action. A reasonable strategy is to first choose shotgun-style air-

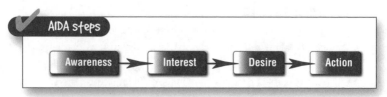

wave and print (magazines, newspapers, billboards, etc.) media to create market awareness. Next, use rifle vehicles like targeted direct mail and tele-prospecting to generate buying interest. Then apply direct sales principles to get customers to the decision to buy. Finally, use interactive media—like the Internet, call centers, or direct response print—to get customers to take action.

As always, effective marketing relies on using the best available tools to influence buying behavior. None of the big four promotional categories are going to disappear anytime soon. Media convergence is a good thing, even for those of us with our livelihoods tied to the direct mail industry. As information continues to migrate from print to the Internet, manuals and catalogs will become thinner and less important. However, the inherent promotional weakness of the e-world means that the demand for promotional printed material will increase, just as Raine Consulting predicts.

PAL POINT... In 1939, *New York Times* predicted that the automatic typewriter was going to make the pen and pencil obsolete. This didn't happen. Sure, the typewriter forced these industries to sharpen their strategies, but they thrived for six more decades and will continue to do so. Now some traditional manufacturers, like the A.T. Cross Pen Company for instance, are making forays into the digital arena with high-tech electronic products. Instead of feeling threatened, let's wish them well.

4

United States Postal Service Mail Classifications and Rates

The USPS offers various rates for delivering mail. This rate structure is dependent upon two factors:

1. Delivery speed and quality. The USPS is betting that customers will pay a premium for quicker and more reliable mail flow.

2. Work sharing. The USPS is willing to offer postal discounts if the customer shares in the preparation and partial delivery of their mail. The better prepared your mail is, the less the Postal Service has to handle it. This reduces USPS processing costs, and mailers that undertake these efforts are offered a lower rate structure.

Service

Most mail entering into the postal mail stream is either entered first class or standard (formerly known as third class). There are other classes of mail such as priority, two-day delivery, and periodical mail, which is a classification for publications. First-class mail can include a single letter that you may send to pay a bill or any other reason. First-class postage can also be used for a multimillion-piece mailing sent by companies wishing to contact prospective and existing customers, but this is very expensive.

Companies can also send the same mass mailing via standard service, thereby reducing postal costs. However, you could not mail an individual piece of mail to your Aunt Edna, for instance; this is because there is a minimum amount of pieces required when using standard service.

The differences between using first-class and standard service primarily are delivery speed and return-to-sender services. First-class mail will get to the designated recipients days faster and will be returned to the sender if the address is improper or undeliverable. Conversely, if standard mail is chosen, errant and otherwise undeliverable mail will not be returned. First-class mailers pay a substantial premium over standard service—about one-third more on average, and even higher in many circumstances. Therefore, cost considerations have to be weighed with the delivery requirements.

Work Sharing

Whether you are mailing first-class or standard service, the USPS will give you discounts on mass mailings if you perform the following services yourself:

1. Put the mail in proper order. This is known as presorting the mail and requires using zip codes and other postal identification codes (i.e., appended carrier route numbers) to properly sequence the mail. Commercial software programs perform this service for high-volume mailers. This software also standardizes addresses for the USPS, which is a requirement, although no specific discount is given for this function.

2. Mail automation. This is known as "barcoding" the mail. Barcodes are applied to the mail in a location where postal machinery can read them and process the mail in a more efficient manner, without worker intervention. These barcodes are developed from the zip code and corresponding delivery

TOM DESTREE
GRAPHIC ARTS TECHNICAL FOUNDATION
200 DEER RUN RD
SEWICKLEY PA   15143-2324

|₁₁₁|₁||₁|₁₁₁₁||₁|₁₁|₁₁|₁||₁₁₁|₁|₁||₁₁|₁|₁₁||₁₁₁₁||₁₁₁₁₁|₁|₁|

point locations. Again, commercial software aids in developing these barcodes, and they can be applied by various variable imaging technologies such as laser, inkjet, and labels.

3. Mail piece design. The USPS will allow you to mail at discounted rates if your mail piece is smaller and weighs less. Physics tells us that smaller and lighter pieces can be handled more efficiently. Therefore, the USPS does not incur the added cost associated with heavier mail and passes some of the savings on to the mailer. The most typical designations are "letter mail" and "flat mail." Letter mail measures up to 11¼×6⅛ in. (286×156 mm), and flat mail measures beyond that. Not surprisingly, letter mail is less expensive to mail than flat mail. In terms of weight, first-class mail costs are increased by ounces. The most common breakpoint for standard mail is approximately 3.2 oz. (91 g). Mail weighing above this point costs more than mail weighing below it.

An additional discount is offered for standard mail. This is known as destination delivery discounts or "drop shipping." Simply put, the USPS offers discounts to mailers that deliver their mail to the various USPS facilities instead of entering it all at a nearby facility. Mailers taking advantage of drop shipping save for both themselves and the USPS.

Additionally, it's important to note that, although no discount is offered, mass first-class mailers are required to run their addresses through a change-of-address program to match their file against the USPS-recorded address changes.

PAL POINT... The concept of work sharing is very important for high-volume mailers. As we discuss at length in the production sections of this book, tremendous savings are available to mailers that undertake some mail preparation tasks themselves. Work sharing is truly a win-win-win proposition —for the client, the mail services company, and the USPS.

Postal Rate Changes: A Fact of Life

We've entered a new postal era. Recently, the USPS has been battling rising labor rates and decreasing revenue—a difficult combination. As a result, postal rate increases have been coming fast and furious, with three rate hikes in two and a half years from January 1999 to July 2001.

The bad news is that some customers may get scared and temporarily reduce the scope of their direct mail programs. The good news is threefold. First, when these same customers discover that their marketing results are suffering, they'll come back. Second, postal rate turbulence means there's a greater need for direct marketers to provide leadership to help customers navigate through direct mail's increasingly choppy waters. Third, marketers will be forced to target more efficiently and effectively, and while not always popular, in the long run, this trend should be good for the direct response industry.

The Mechanics of Postal Rate Increases

A postal rate increase begins when the USPS submits a rate increase proposal. Then the Postal Rate Commission (PRC) reviews the USPS operating budget, makes changes as it sees fit, and submit its recommendations to the Postal Board of Governors. For example, the January 2001 rate increase (R-2000) was filed on January 11, 2000, reviewed by the PRC within a few weeks, and ruled on by the PRC in November. Nearly a year after it was first submitted, the new postal rates were implemented on January 7, 2001.

If recent history is any predictor of the future, the differential between USPS requests and actual approved final rates can be quite large. The USPS doesn't always get what it asks for. Neither the PRC nor the Board of Governors has been shy about changing USPS plans set before them. In the January 1999 postal increase, the USPS got about half of what it wanted, pretty much across the board.

Likely areas where the USPS, the PRC, and the Board of Governors will be looking for future rate cases are:

• **Automation.** The USPS recently asked for rate increases for automated mail of nearly 15%. At the same time, basic mail (which requires the most manual postal effort) went up only 2%. The logic behind this is that the USPS believes they can automate this mail without a pre-applied barcode. However, this automation disincentive is the wrong message for the USPS to send and at some point should be reversed.

• **Drop shipping.** The USPS "passed through" only about 65% of Standard A postal savings generated by drop shipping. This means that a good portion of the projected rate increase could be absorbed by proper recognition of the work-sharing discount. Shouldn't automation-friendly mailers that drop-ship in order to help the USPS meet mail delivery obligations be rewarded with pass-through rates closer to 100%? This is an area that probably will be given careful consideration.

• **Inappropriate rate reductions.** Three times in a row, the USPS asked for rate reductions for mail that falls between 3.3 oz. (94 g) and 16 oz. (454 g). Up to 3.9 oz. (111 g), the average rate of increase is 5%. Then as mail gets progressively heavier, the rate actually decreases until the 1-lb. weight limit is reached. The last two times the USPS asked for similar rate reductions, the PRC threw them out. Hopefully the USPS will stop asking for rate reductions in this class of mail.

The Bottom Line

Direct mailing professionals should count on automated standard mail rates to continue to increase. This means you need to get a better bang for your promotional buck and mail smarter by:

- Better targeting
- Better capturing of automation discounts
- Better creativity

First, better targeting means improving data collection, analysis, and usage. Data cleansing processes must improve so that more mail gets to the right destinations and is put in the hands of key businesspeople with influence. Second, since better targeting usually results in smaller-sized mailings, direct mailers are likely to lose some valuable automation discounts. If your number of mail pieces within a zip code drops below 150 addresses, you will sacrifice the favorable five-digit postal rate. Since the gap between the three- and five-digit rates likely will keep on increasing, it's more important than ever to get comfortable with commingling technology to achieve maximum postal discounts. Third, your creative work is vital to future success. Use good test marketing principles before rolling out expensive direct mail campaigns. Commingling test runs with other mail will help reduce your overall mailing costs.

PAL POINT... For now, it's smart to keep an ear to the ground about future postal rate increases. Around the turn of the decade, *The Kiplinger Letter* forecast a 50-cent first-class stamp by 2006. Don't expect first-class mail to absorb the bulk of the increasing postal deficit. Position yourself as an industry resource and help navigate reasonable courses of action for your clients. Get ready—for better or worse, postal increases are a continuing reality.

Set Realistic Mailing Objectives

When beginning a direct mail project, envision what you want to achieve. As Steven Covey rightly points out, "Begin with the end in mind." Know the goals of each and every project you're working on and make sure they're realistic.

For example, is it realistic to sell a $20,000 networking solution from a $1.50 mailing? No, but a $100 software program may be. How about a $2,000 furnace? No. But getting prospects to visit an informational we   ͏   ͏ existing customers to schedule a $75 furn

What about selling a luxury car with   no! However, it is a reasonable goal to get potential ͏u͏, ͏ into showrooms for test-drives. Jaguar did just this when they sent out 110,000 highly personalized direct mail packages to an upscale target audience. Those who test-drove a Jaguar as a result of this direct mail promotion were given a die-cast model Jaguar worth $80. (Of course the out-of-pocket cost was less.) As a direct result, hundreds of automobiles were sold.

How do the economics of direct mail work for low-cost items? Let's consider magazine subscriptions, where the costs of acquiring new subscribers is higher than the total first year's revenue? When you consider the lifetime value of customers, then direct mail subscription programs make sense. If you keep track of all results and associated costs, you will know your payback period. As you experiment with new components and program design changes, you can always measure results against the control piece and make good promotional decisions.

Focus on Expected Results

Let's get back to the luxury car. Did you know that on average, every person who walks into a car dealership has $400,000 of lifetime purchases written on his or her forehead? Getting people into the dealer's door is what makes sense. If you modify your objective to getting qualified potential buyers into dealerships, you will experience better and more realistic results. Project champions should think of the lifetime value of a customer, regardless of whether the product is liquor, cars, credit cards, or almost anything else. Once the scope of the project is properly defined, all that needs to be done is to focus on implementation.

What if you're trying to sell magazines? If you look at the cost of subscription acquisition as a percentage of the actual product itself, you can set targets that have an acceptable payback period. Then you will know an appropriate size budget and work within those constraints. Most direct mailings need to be profit-motivated with an acceptable return generated from every investment.

PAL POINT... Once a program's goals are completely defined, it's time to start exploring different designs, copy, and direct mail solutions that will achieve the stated objectives.

Direct Mail Program Planning

Project lead times seem to shrink every year. Effective data controls will increase the speed of your data processing and get your materials in the mail stream faster. Cost is more important than ever. Front-end data management will decrease data production time and save you money. Mailings that use multiple lists will benefit from back-end data analysis so future mailings can be smaller, yet still achieve the same number of responses. Put all these ingredients together in an effective customer relationship marketing (CRM) program.

Key Ingredients for Successful Programs

The first step in any direct mail project, regardless of whether it's part of a CRM program, should be the identification of your target market and desired results. Many project designs would run better and cheaper if minor adjustments had been made *at the beginning* of creative development. Therefore, a direct marketing technical team—with data processing, imaging, bindery, lettershop, and response management expertise—should be present at all program development meetings.

Establish a realistic critical path. Once a project's goals have been agreed upon, clearly communicate them to all appropriate people. Unless your internal and external business partners know your project's goals, their ability to help you is limited.

Make your data file structure uniform and use industry standard media formats. Prior to handing off the project to your data house, create a data file layout. Without this, your supplier will need to decipher one, which takes time and increases your chances of error. A data file layout includes elements such as name and address components, list identifier codes, telephone numbers (for tandem telemarketing), account numbers, as well as other demographic and psychographic pieces of information. Then, provide your supplier with detailed instructions (data specification logic) enabling programmers to clean up your database exactly the way you want.

Before beginning a direct mail CRM campaign, project champions need to clearly define the desired response they want from mail recipients. If getting people into a showroom is the goal, the program should be designed one way. If it's to get families to remove existing pizza magnets from their refrigerators and put up yours instead, your program needs to be designed another way. If you're soliciting on the behalf of a nonprofit charitable organization, you will need yet a different set of goals.

Once goals are identified and agreed upon, it is the role of the project champion to ensure that continuity is built into a program. As in direct sales, where sales representatives need to call on prospects seven times on average before reaching the first sale, direct mail isn't too different. While some people will respond to the first piece of mail they receive, many others need to be exposed to the message several times before they feel compelled to take the desired action. "One-Shot-Charlie" type mailings rarely influence enough people the first time to make the program cost-effective. Startup costs—which may include list acquisition, design costs, and production inefficiencies—need to be amortized over repeat mailings to be cost-effective.

An Example
In the late 1990s, a pharmaceutical company had ambitions of developing a newsletter full of useful information targeted toward people suffering from a specific allergy-related medical problem. The pharmaceutical company didn't know

much about direct mail design, but at least it did know it wanted subscription growth, market awareness, sales generation, and measurable results. To start with, the pharmaceutical company had a fledgling database of about 15,000 carefully selected recipients, but no realistic knowledge of where the program could go and what it could be used to achieve. The company thought that the information-laden newsletter could trigger sales and retain existing customers, but wasn't sure. The pharmaceutical company contracted the project out to SMR/Tytrek, which helped to design a complete direct mail loop that included mail, analysis, redesign, re-mail, more analysis, and so forth.

The results were tracked through a few complete cycles, and the pharmaceutical company discovered exactly what information each recipient needed. Then it was able to appropriately customize the newsletter for individual readers. The company solicited feedback in several ways, but the most effective method turned out to be a perforated reply card. Soon all of its newsletters contained this response device. Results were tracked, and within a few short months, the company had gathered a mountain of information from the newsletter, website, and other advertising activities. In all, data for 200,000 targeted recipients was captured, after removing duplicate and undeliverable records. This information was kept current and, within a short period of time, became a valuable source of business.

Additionally, SMR/Tytrek was solicited for design advice. As a result, some highly effective promotional pieces were developed and distributed to segments of the client's self-developed "house" data file, which further augmented the program's success. To streamline the process of capturing information written on returned reply cards, the company used inside/outside inkjet imaging technology, which reduced the amount of handwriting that needed to be read. Better information led to better results, which in turn led to better information. This is the kind of vicious cycle that clients like. Now that they've tasted real success, this pharmaceutical company intends on continuing this database effort, in addition to doing everything else right on the list acquisition and testing side.

Here's a last footnote regarding this pharmaceutical company. It asked the question, "How could the success of this program be parlayed to other products and areas of the company?" The goal no longer was whether direct mail would work, but how the company can best showcase total company strengths to achieve goals across other business units as well. The pharmaceutical company was so pleased with its results that it rolled out similar programs in other areas with much larger sales volumes and much more ambitious mailing sizes. These types of excellent results are a byproduct of well-thought-out job planning early in the development of the project.

PAL POINT... Repetition, two-way communication, and program continuity are at the core of an effective CRM (customer relationship marketing) program. It's vital that direct marketers think about lifetime relationships as they conceive and manage their various projects. How can a solicitation for a magazine at an 80% discount pay for itself unless a relationship with a subscriber is maintained beyond the trial membership period? Not surprisingly, it can't. Repetitive contact is what makes many types of mailings pay off. Seasoned direct mailing professionals usually think of direct mail programs in terms of years, not weeks or months. Only then are their expectations realistic and successful.

CHAPTER 8

Account Management

If you enjoy working with a wide variety of people, crave being in the center of the action, and thrive in a fast-paced work environment, then direct mail account management may be just your ticket. Salespeople bring in the work. Production makes it. Account managers ensure that everything is done right and on time. Although a lot of people with different functional responsibilities need to work in harmony to produce direct mail jobs on time and on budget, let's focus on account management. This role in direct mail services is quite different than in most other industries.

Overview

Account managers are a vital communication link between the customer and internal production. All requests from customers should be channeled through this department. A good policy is to not allow work to be scheduled without first being assigned an account manager.

To succeed, account managers must:

- Have a complete understanding of the client job specifications
- Communicate clearly and effectively, both verbally and in writing
- Be able to process all detailed, complex ideas and requests
- Manage a multitude of jobs, processes, and paperwork in a timely and organized manner
- Follow a job's progress throughout the production process
- Immediately notify sales representatives and other key personnel of any delays or significant challenges

Account managers should think of their function as being both "vendor" and "customer" to their internal and external customers. As a customer, account managers must treat everyone with dignity and respect and be fully prepared when discussing or handing-off jobs. They should put all requests or job changes in writing and ask for the same in return. When problems occur, it's important to keep the management team fully aware of what's happening.

As a vendor, account managers can never forget that, since they are authorized representatives of their employer, they must treat all customers with dignity and respect. They should request all information or specifications in writing and provide the same. Job processing documentation must be prepared and kept up to date so that nothing falls through the cracks. When problems occur, it's much better to let your customers know sooner rather than later, especially if delivery dates are in jeopardy. And, like a good salesperson, it's important to know your customers' goals and work to achieve them in partnership.

Take Personal Responsibility

Some customers require more involvement than others. Some ask their assigned account managers to provide more support and marketing guidance in conjunction with project management tasks. Seasoned account managers know that each client has different expectations. To provide the right amount of support, account managers should look to the sales representatives that they work with for guidance.

It is important to keep in mind that each job and client is the ultimate responsibility of the assigned account manager. Account managers must check the quality of the jobs throughout each stage of the manufacturing process. Account managers function as the "eyes and ears" for their customers while their jobs are in house. The levels of attention that account managers pay to their jobs and the type of communication style that they use will ultimately determine the success or failure of the customer relationship. Anticipating potential problems and following up on every promise and concern is essential to ensuring customer satisfaction. Decision-making speed and consistent good judgment are key success factors.

Consider yourself and your company to be in partnership with your customers. Learn what their goals are and work to achieve them. Providing quality account management and support services goes a long way toward creating extended profitable relationships. Perhaps customers will name your company as their preferred vendor.

Account managers must be available to their customers. It is important that they quickly and courteously respond to telephone messages, pages, and emails. Unresponsiveness is extremely frustrating to customers, destroys confidence, and threatens business relationships—even long-term ones. Be diligent in returning all communications in a timely manner.

Information and Specifications

When receiving job instructions and specifications, account managers must invest the proper amount of time to completely understand each project. It is important that they receive complete written instructions from the client. If they are missing, it is their responsibility to get them. Without consistent and accurate data, it's impossible to do a good job. The account management team leader should develop written procedures and create a job checklist to help account managers make sure that they have all the detailed information they need. As your company's services evolve, these procedures and checklists should be updated as necessary.

It is the duty of the account manager to fully understand every job on which they work, and this means understanding the ultimate goal or output of each one. Without a complete understanding of the "final destination," it is difficult to produce the job correctly or get it there on time. It is critical that account managers clearly and accurately interpret job information and hand off jobs to other departments with unambiguous directions. Particular attention should be paid to communicating any expectations that are unique to the job. When dealing with internal data service departments, an easy and effective way to communicate job requirements is to use flowcharts. These flowcharts can be simple or elaborate, depending upon the processes required.

Job Changes

In the direct mail industry, change is constant. While working on jobs, frequently you will receive requests to change or modify the original order. These changes must be submitted in writing, and they should be clear, understandable, and plainly written. Since customer relationships are so important, avoid verbal changes whenever possible. Of utmost importance: Make sure your internal and external clients know that changes or modifications can cause the project to be delayed and may increase costs. You may need to renegotiate the due date and/or job pricing. Don't forget to involve the salesperson in this process, modify all internal paperwork, and properly redistribute the revised job order. Since more internal coordination is necessary, errors are more likely when job changes occur than when they don't. So try to get it right the first time.

Communication

—with Frank Shear, President, Seaboard Bindery

Success in the direct mail world depends on choosing the right paper, layout, printing, binding, and personalization methods, right? Is this all? Not unless you want to ignore the most valuable key success factor: good communication.

Today's direct mail professionals are stretched so thinly that they must rely on their suppliers to guide them through the complicated buying process. The best direct mail companies help customers maneuver around landmines and achieve their business goals. Let your partners help you in the same way. In addition to simply faxing over job specifications, pick up the phone and discuss your project. Good communication allows you to reduce costs, eliminate frustration, and be a hero in the eyes of your customers.

If direct mailing services customers supply all their vendors (up and down the direct mail supply chain) with accurate and timely information, everyone's lives will be less stressful. The number of problems will be reduced, customer satisfaction will rise, production costs will be lower, and profits will be higher. When job specifications are unclear, questions go unanswered and production problems increase exponentially.

Data processing companies, lettershops, and binderies want to be valuable information resources for their customers, but effective two-way information flow is needed to achieve this lofty goal. Before direct mail professionals can present alternative solutions to their customers, they need information about a job's end-use. They need to know the minutia of your job to be of the greatest value to you. In short, your suppliers depend on good communication and information flow.

Begin with the End in Mind

The best printing layout isn't necessarily the most efficient mail or bindery layout. For example, if a job is bindery-intensive, it may be in the mailer's best interest to change the layout to save on outsourcing costs and production time. Sometimes one-up layouts are best, and sometimes multiple-up ones are best. Working in a vacuum can be terribly inefficient and costly.

Minor product design changes might allow machines to run faster and reduce spoilage. The bottom line? There are definitely times when a little more should be spent on print-ing to save in the bindery or lettershop, or vice versa. But this discovery process can only start with good two-way communication. Work backwards through the supply chain to ensure product and process efficiency.

Scheduling

Direct mail project leaders shouldn't wait until their job is printed before contacting their lettershop or bindery repre-sentative. Scheduling conflicts are a way of life in the direct mail world, and the best way to ensure that your due date is met is to schedule your job well in advance. Good suppliers of direct mail services know that problems happen and do their best to accommodate minor changes to schedules.

When Sending a Job

Before placing a job, write an instruction sheet for each sup-plier explaining what you want done, along with a sample. You may not know when or how this minor time invest-ment will help you, but it will. No one is as familiar with your requirements as you are, and what seems obvious to you may not be to someone else. Purchase orders are cer-tainly preferred, but at the very least, describe what opera-tions need to be done and define success. Think of your job from the perspective of someone who has never heard of your client and doesn't know what items are on the "must" list.

It's uncomfortable for a manufacturing company to have an important production question regarding a rush job and not be able to get an answer. When in this awkward position, suppliers have two choices: either wait for information and miss the deadline or make an unauthorized production decision. Either way, they risk incurring the wrath of their customers if they are wrong. Jobs with quick turnaround times and poorly communicated instructions are disasters waiting to happen.

PAL POINT... Help your supply chain help you. In today's fast-paced business environment, one unplanned detail can break the proverbial camel's back. Good communication with all involved companies will make your life easier and increase your profits in the hectic direct mail world.

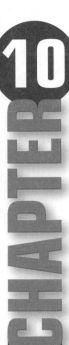

10

Electronic Updates: The Wave of the Future

Wouldn't it be easy for clients if their mailing services partners offered daily electronic job status updates on large-volume jobs? Wouldn't a lot of time-wasting telephone tag be avoided? More and more lettershops think so. Although the direct mail industry hasn't yet reached the FedEx standard for information on demand, that day may not be far away.

In our detail-oriented direct mail industry, accurate and timely information is critically important. Project success depends on gathering the right information and making the right decisions. During the 1990s, a lot of people decreased their telephone usage in favor of email, but communication still originated when customers made inquiries. The best suppliers proactively provided customers with status updates as best they could, but without automated systems, problems still fell through the cracks.

Fast forward to today. Technology has blazed new trails that make mailing customers' lives easier. Progressive high-volume lettershops now offer clients current job status via email before the working day starts. Typical information includes inventory and production rate data, as well as benchmark goals.

Core Benefits of an Electronic Update System

Inventory. Assume you're working on a million-piece mailing with a dozen different components for a client. If an email inventory status arrives each morning, you'll immediately know if you should be concerned about any aspect of the job. What if your daily report shows that the lettershop received 250,000 each of four different colored envelopes yesterday? What if you need 500,000 blue envelopes?

Instantly, you'd know you have a problem on your hands. Without the update, it's likely you wouldn't have learned of this situation until later on—and possibly too late to do anything about it.

Delivery dates. Electronic information updating systems allow you to carefully monitor your production counts. Assume you've promised your customer an eight-day turn-around time on a million-piece mailing. If your production department averages 100,000 pieces on each of the first four days, you can and should ask how the deadline will be met. Again, under the old information paradigm, you may not discover this situation until it's too late to do anything. With daily electronic updates, you're armed with enough information to ask the right questions and let your customers know you have a potential problem on your hands, if it gets to that.

Benchmarking. Production counts by themselves are good, but not good enough. The best daily electronic status update systems also include production benchmarks. If your morning email shows that your lettershop has planned to produce 100,000 pieces on each of the first six production days, and 200,000 on days seven and eight, then you'll know that you're right on schedule.

PAL POINT... It's a waste of time to ask for data that should be supplied to you in the first place. In this day and age, information should literally be at your fingertips so you have more time to focus on what's truly important—making informed decisions. Is the mailing services industry operating at the FedEx standard yet? Unfortunately, the answer is no. However, some leading companies have their eye on completely auto-mated systems that allow customers to retrieve information on secure sites whenever they want. As an industry, we're not there yet...but just wait.

11 CHAPTER

Testing

One of the truest maxims of the direct mail business is "test, test, and then test some more." Some of the most effective direct marketers seem to be decidedly understated about the importance of creativity. They know that great results don't necessarily follow from the flashiest or most graphically challenging campaigns. Instead, if a dull-looking campaign performs better during a test, they chuck the award winner and follow the pieces with better results.

If this sounds paradoxical, it shouldn't. Direct marketing isn't about winning industry awards. Rather, it's about being detached enough to remove one's own design preferences and having the discipline to stick with what works. If your superb-looking new creative design doesn't out-pull the control product, you should either change it and try again or put the concept out to pasture. In direct mail the only thing that counts is results. Woe be to the direct marketer who ignores this time-tested lesson. The best continuing direct mail programs are those that constantly test a single changing condition and incorporate the changes that work and set aside the ones that don't. In this way, smart marketers produce the best performing pieces with repeatable results.

Industry legend David Olgivy describes the testing process this way in *Olgivy on Advertising*:

> You can test every variable in your mailings and determine exactly its effect on your sales. But because you can only test one variable at a time, you cannot afford to test them all. So you have to choose which to test. Experienced practitioners always test some variables, but seldom those that experience has taught them make little difference in results. Next to the positioning of your product,

the most important variables to be tested are pricing, terms of payment, premiums, and the format of your mailing.

Asking for the full price and cash with the order will reduce the number of people who respond. But it may turn up more customers who are likely to stay with you over the years. Only testing will tell. The more you test, the more profitable your direct mail will become.

Once you have evolved a mailing that produces profitable results, treat it as a "control" and start testing ways to beat it. Try adding a premium, or putting in an expiration date, or adding enclosures—like a personalized letter from your president. They cost money, but if they increase your profit, why worry?

Sometimes an expensive control can be made less expensive without reducing your orders. You can test a smaller mailing piece, or eliminate the brochure altogether. You may be in for a pleasant surprise. Less can be more.

PAL POINT... Don't assume anything. Test every component of your mailing. Test the envelope copy, color, and graphics. Test inserts, letter copy, letter length, headlines, signatures, messages, and offers. Test fonts, graphics, premiums, attachments, bindery processes, and labels. Test different lists, demographics, and psychographics. Don't assume. *Test*.

Quality Assurance

Without quality, you don't have a product. Successful direct mail service providers define, measure, audit, and analyze quality. Although admittedly a daunting task, designing effective quality assurance systems and procedures is well worth the effort. Before outsourcing your next direct mail job, ask existing and potential suppliers about their approach to quality assurance. You will make better outsourcing decisions.

Quality involves everyone within an organization—from production workers to company presidents. Quality is not what customers expect; it's what manufacturers inspect. The backbone of a good quality assurance program is accountability. If employees believe that their mistakes either don't matter or will be caught by other people, complacency and lack of attention to detail will be the logical result. Quality assurance is a balancing act. When taken to ridiculous levels, unrealistic quality fanaticism kills output and profitability.

One challenge the direct mail production industry faces is that every piece of mail is different. Therefore, we must question everything. If operators don't see a barcode, they need to look at the job jacket instructions to see if it's missing. If they see a barcode, they also need to look at the job jacket to verify image positioning. Get the point? Either way, they've got to look at the job jacket. Direct mail production occurs in a variable job shop manufacturing environment. This is quite different from our cousins in the printing and binding industries. There, conformity is the goal and success depends on every piece being the same. Those of us in direct mail production deal with constantly changing parameters, which is exactly the opposite of stasis.

Quality Assurance Needs
Great Information Systems

A company's choice of job definition/production workflow software is critically important to future success. Consistent product quality depends on accurate job definitions and unambiguous communication between departments. High-volume mail service providers need integrated software systems that:

- Disseminate the right information to the right departments
- Determine the shortest manufacturing critical paths
- Integrate production schedules with other work in house
- Track material flow
- Monitor production on a real-time basis

No two customers are alike. People provide information in different ways, and it's up to account managers to get varying information into a standard, familiar format, easily understood by everyone. Good software standardizes and disperses customer instructions to the right people throughout a manufacturing facility.

Operating procedures are also necessary, and one prevented a major headache for the company of one of the authors. Harte-Hanks Baltimore requires employees to fan through boxes of inserts before loading pockets. One of their financial services clients offers different credit card interest rates to groups of people with different credit ratings. Since insert examination is an item on our standard production checklist, our diligent employee noticed that many boxes contained inserts with different interest rate offers. He stopped the job from being run—all employees are empowered to do this—and prevented a mailing that could have had dire consequences for the client.

Data Audit

Your mailing services company should sample converted data before beginning production. These "data audits" usually involve random sampling by extracting records from the outgoing data file and examining them for conformity to customer expectations. Everything is checked including data field content (i.e., zip code, customer ID, ordering history, etc.), uppercase and lowercase use, barcoding, data truncation, and so forth.

If a data audit reveals a problem, it's important to determine where it occurred. Most mail houses start at the end of the data conversion process and work backwards by examining the printing program, output file (post-data conversion), and input file (pre-data conversion)—in that order. For example, if a data audit reveals a truncating problem, we may discover that a computer operator picked up data from byte positions 15 to 20 instead of from 15 to 30. Although fixing a problem such as this consumes additional resources, at least the mailing will not have been produced incorrectly.

Interval Sampling

It's hard to imagine a quality assurance program without good sampling and inspection procedures. Standards must be defined in all production departments and may differ, even within the same job. Some operations are susceptible to manufacturing problems and high spoilage rates, while others run great for days, weeks, and months on end. Understandably, problem-prone manufacturing areas require more frequent sample inspection. Customer requirements and job quantities also are important factors in determining appropriate sampling intervals.

Quality assurance needs machine operators armed with clearly written job jacket instructions regarding sampling frequency and product expectations. These operators are the frontlines that pull samples, inspect the work, and record their findings. The next quality assurance layer involves production monitors who constantly inspect recent sample pulls. Stage three involves gathering, examining, recording, and storing samples. The last step is the account manager who shoulders ultimate responsibility for customer expectation compliance.

Analysis: Seeing the Big Picture

Deconstructing problems and analyzing results is vital to manufacturing performance and customer satisfaction. Good companies analyze production data and determine whether overall quality is trending in the right direction. Not only do they examine historical data, they consider other information such as out-of-pocket rework costs, wasted production hours, and percentage of on-time deliveries.

Analysis allows mailing service providers to recognize when error patterns emerge. If errors are sporadically dispersed throughout a plant, they're probably okay. However, detectable patterns of problems may be indicative of a systemic breakdown somewhere. Regardless, it's important to study available data and make better decisions based on past history.

Plotting sample frequency graphs is an underutilized management tool. For example, if a mailing services company produces a million-piece job with imprinted unique barcodes, they could scan each sample, determine when it was produced, and plot the results in a graph. Large gaps between plotted points would indicate that someone didn't do his or her job properly. As long as a reasonable shop floor data capture system exists, isolating and researching data anomalies is easy.

The two most dangerous types of employees are those who can't follow instructions and those who can only follow instructions. It's unrealistic to believe that you or anyone else can write procedures that will cover all or even most manufacturing contingencies. The bottom line is that job shop manufacturers need people who can think.

PAL POINT... There is the saying "if you find your mistake, it's not a mistake." The logical corollary is this: "If someone else finds your mistake, then it's a mistake." Quality assurance begins with each individual and radiates throughout an organization. It requires well-thought-out management procedures and information technologies. No matter which tools are best suited for a particular manufacturing facility, they must improve job definition, measurement, auditing, and analysis. Quality assurance helps companies keep their promises. Isn't this the point of being in business?

SECTION 2

Direct Mail Pre-Production

Production Friendly Direct Mail Layouts

There's a time and place for eye-popping, unusual direct mail designs, but most of the time, direct mailing professionals need to produce good projects at the lowest possible cost. Achieving production efficiencies depends on starting with machine capabilities firmly in mind and working backward to arrive at production friendly layouts.

For example, when planning laser-personalized direct mail projects, pay attention to mailing equipment limitations because some formats are more conducive to long production runs than others. It's so easy for designers to wistfully add a ¼ in. (6 mm) here and an ⅛ in. (3 mm) there without realizing they're dramatically increasing their production costs. Production unfriendly layouts can waste a lot of paper, machine time, effort, and energy while increasing manufacturing costs and blowing deadlines. Unless there's a very good reason to do otherwise, high-volume mailing professionals should design their projects so they conform to common machine specifications.

Efficient Direct Mail Cutoff Sizes

Inches	Millimeters
5½	140
5⅗	142
5⅔	144
7	178
7⅓	186
8½	216
9⅓	237
11	279
14	356
17	432
22	559
28	711

Common Press Sizes

Some people think that efficient production is limited to the printing press's cylinder circumference divided by two, which, in the case of the most common direct mail machine (22 in., 559 mm), results in an 11-in. (279-mm) cutoff. This is wrong. Cutoffs of 7⅓ in. (186 mm) or even 5½ in. (140 mm) are just as efficient on a 22-

in. cylinder. When planning product sizes, take your cylinder's circumference and divide evenly. Just because 11-in. products are so prevalent doesn't mean you have to limit yourself to this size; 14 in. (356 mm), 17 in. (432 mm), and all their derivative sizes are just as efficient to produce.

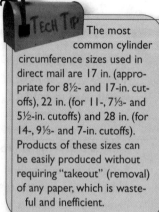

The circumference of the printing press cylinder determines efficient cutoff sizes. For example, a cylinder with a 28-in. (711-mm) circumference is efficient for 14-in. (28 ÷ 2), 9⅓-in. (28 ÷ 3), and 7-in. (28 ÷ 4) products. If your direct mail piece needs to be just a little taller than 8½ in. (216 mm), you might as well design it to have a height of 9⅓ in. (237 mm) instead of 8¾ in. (222 mm) or any other production unfriendly size. If you make a mistake and design a piece with a height of 9½ in. (241 mm), then you must use an 11-in. (279 mm) form, which wastes 13.6% of the available paper and slows down production as well.

Production Inefficiencies Caused by Takeout

A lot of direct mail work is finished on bow-style document conversion machines. Two important settings on document converters determine (1) how far paper advances and (2) how much "takeout" is required. A major production bottleneck is knife-cutting speed. If an 11-in. (279-mm) form without bleeds is being produced on a 22-in. (559-mm) circumference cylinder, the knife only needs to make one cut per form. However, if you have a production unfriendly format of 9½ in. (241 mm), for example, you need a 1½-in. (38-mm) takeout between forms. This requires the knife to travel twice, slowing down production by at least 30%. Moreover, you'll be wasting about 15% of your time on printing presses and laser imagers because only 19 in. (483 mm) of the available 22-in. circumference will be imaged. Bottom line: It's very important to avoid takeouts when designing high-volume mail projects.

The width of the form is important too. The maximum roll width on most laser imaging machines is 18 in. (457 mm). After allowing for two ½-in. (13-mm) pin-feed strips, designers have a 17-in. (432-mm) roll width available for image use. Eliminating paper width roll waste is easy—just decrease the width of the paper roll. (Note: Ordering special roll sizes from the mill may cost more and take longer to receive.) However, you're paying for production on 18-in.-wide machines, meaning that even though you're only using a 15-in. (381-mm) roll, you're still paying 18-in. machine rates for both printing presses and laser imagers. As with height, don't forget you can run your forms multiple-wide. In the case of an 18-in. roll (17-in. image area), 17-, 8½-, and 5⅔-in.-wide (432, 216, and 144-mm-wide) forms all maximize roll width.

Image Rotation: An Example of a 16% Productivity Gain

In certain circumstances, rotating your image 90° will save you time and money. Consider a 17-in.-tall form that is 7⅓ in. wide. If you run this project two-up on a 17-in. circumference cylinder, you will need a 15⅔-in.-wide paper roll (7⅓ in. × 2, plus 1 in. for pin-feed holes). For every 17 in. of

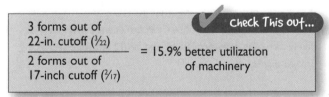

$$\frac{\text{3 forms out of 22-in. cutoff } (3\!/\!22)}{\text{2 forms out of 17-inch cutoff } (2\!/\!17)} = 15.9\% \text{ better utilization of machinery}$$

Check This out...

paper length, you'll get two forms out. Instead, rotate your image 90° to get three forms out of a 22-in. cylinder—a perfect fit resulting in a productivity gain of nearly 16%.

There are other benefits too. For example, you'll be folding your forms with the paper grain—which makes a significant

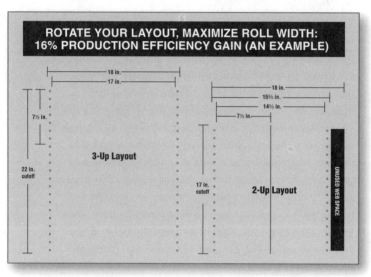

ROTATE YOUR LAYOUT, MAXIMIZE ROLL WIDTH: 16% PRODUCTION EFFICIENCY GAIN (AN EXAMPLE)

quality difference on heavier stocks. And you're being charged for less printing footage while maximizing the width of the machine. If you're paying your laser personalization services company $1.50/M an inch, you will now get a form every 7⅓ in. (186 mm) instead of every 8½ in. (216 mm), which amounts to roughly $1.75/M in laser imaging and $1.00/M in printing costs. In addition, there's the chance that ordering a special roll width will increase your paper costs a bit too. Let's put it all together. Rotating the image and shifting production to a 22-in. circumference cylinder will likely save you between $3/M and $4/M without sacrificing image quality.

How you finish your projects is important too. For example, assume you need an 8½×11-in. (216×279-mm) personalized letter and a 3½×8½-in. (89×216-mm) reply device. If you run it on a 14-in. (356-mm) form, gatefold it, and slit it to the head, you will get a personalized letter and a freestanding, nested personalized reply device. Although gatefolding costs more than standard folding, it is far less expensive than outsourcing a matched mailing...with far fewer headaches. If you are producing a toner-only form, then offset printing isn't needed, thereby removing cutoff limitations. Combining black-only printing with holograms and Label-Aire applications may be a good way to achieve the design flexibility you need without sacrificing production speed.

PAL POINT... There are a lot of direct mail machines out there. For our purposes, we've limited our discussions to the most widely available cylinder sizes. If you look hard enough, you may be able to find someone with 10- or 30-in. (254- or 762-mm) cylinder circumferences, but these are few and far between.

Postal Friendly Envelope Design

Direct mail projects won't be successful unless they're well planned. This includes paying attention to every detail, right down to individual mail components. Envelope selection is very important for two reasons: marketing effectiveness and production efficiency. With so much marketplace emphasis on cost containment, we'll concentrate on production efficiencies today.

Choose the right envelope for your next mailing. With proper training, direct mail project managers are able to foresee and avoid most envelope-related problems.

Window Envelopes

When a mailing suffers from poor production rates, the envelope window is often the culprit. Direct mail production companies prefer envelopes with cellophane windows instead of "open" (cellophane-less) ones because they are less susceptible to having inserts catch and rip on the windows. Even if open envelopes successfully make it through lettershop production, they are still more likely to get caught in USPS processing equipment than their cellophane counterparts. Open envelopes cost a bit less, but their increased production risk almost always outweighs this insignificant benefit.

If your mailing uses window-less envelopes, a potential problem still may lurk. As one would expect, white envelopes with addresses in black ink have wonderful "reflectance" properties. On the other hand, colored envelopes need either a knocked-out or high-contrast area for the address. The *USPS Domestic Mail Manual* (DMM) is very specific about reflectance requirements for postal automation compatibility. For example, blue envelopes with black barcodes may fail the reflectance test and should definitely be tested prior to production. When using white envelopes with windows, reflectance may still be a problem if addressed inserts have interfering ghosted images, patterns, or dark colors. When in doubt, show your local postal official the design early during the job planning stage.

Side-Seam vs. V-style Envelopes

For large-volume jobs running on high-speed inserting equipment, choose side-seam style envelopes with flat flaps.

The distance these flaps must travel during the opening and sealing processes determines production rates. In the past, V-style envelopes didn't hamper production too much because previous generation "swing-arm" style equipment was slow.

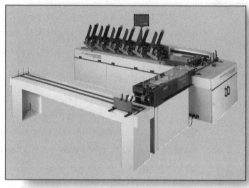

FlowMaster 12000 inserter. *Courtesy Sure-Feed Engineering, Inc.*

However, today's high-speed FlowMaster-style inserting machinery can achieve productivity gains of 50% or more

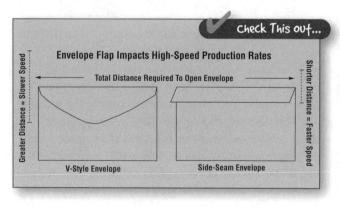

Direct Mail Pal

when side-seam envelopes are used. Although side-seam envelopes cost a bit more, associated production savings are more than enough compensation to lower your project's overall cost.

Tap Test

To qualify for postal automation discounts, addressed inserts must properly lie within their envelopes. Mailings need to pass a "tap" test in which the postal barcode remains fully exposed as sealed samples are tapped from the bottom and both sides, jogging all contents in three directions. As each side is tapped, a ⅛-in. (3-mm) minimum clearance distance must be maintained between the postal barcode on the insert and all edges of the window.

Although always important, this tap test is especially critical for thick mailings. Envelopes need to be opened wider than usual to accommodate a lot of inserted material. Since this mechanical action temporarily reduces envelope width by pulling in the upper corners, production rates usually depend on slightly undersized insert widths. However, undersized inserts shift more within sealed envelopes, making the left-right tap test increasingly important as mailings get thicker.

Envelope Potpourri

• Make sure your envelope manufacturer packs its products tightly. If lettershops are forced to use sagging, bowing, or otherwise imperfect envelopes, turnaround times, production costs, and spoilage rates will be disappointing.

Tech Tip
For wet-applied "live" stamp jobs, make sure your lettershop is careful about moisture seepage because remoistenable glue strips can be unintentionally activated. Pressure-sensitive stamps eliminate this risk and are highly preferred.

• To qualify for maximum postal discounts, envelopes must comply with USPS and CPC aspect ratio standards. Although most standard envelope sizes comply, still it's best to reference the DMM before beginning unusual-sized projects.

• If you want "flat" (8½×11-in. or similar) mailings to be automatically inserted, choose oversized envelopes with flaps running lengthwise.

• Envelope coatings can cause adhesion problems. Adhesive technology is part art and part science. The only way to be certain that glue and inkjet ink will properly adhere to coated surfaces is to run tests before beginning production.

PAL POINT... Be careful when using old envelopes. Remoistenable glue is formulated to react quickly to the presence of moisture and may dry out if too much time passes before use.

15

Data Processing: Format and Record Layout

Smooth data processing can be the difference between successful and unsuccessful mailing campaigns. Although technological advances have dramatically changed the direct mail landscape, cost-effective mailing programs still begin with good front-end data management.

Direct mail's future has never been brighter. The demand for direct mail is still increasing because it is non-invasive, user-friendly, reliable, and highly effective. Managing the complicated front-end data processing procedure under severe time constraints is an important key success factor in today's fast-paced business environment. Project managers should rely on their direct mail services company for data preparation expertise and involve them early in the design phase of any job.

The road to data preparation hell is paved with good intentions. Although large-volume mailing customers often try to process their data to a particular mailing company's standards, rarely is much time or money saved; instead, duplication of effort occurs. Out of necessity, most sophisticated direct mailing services companies have developed "house" data formats, which allow incoming data to be formatted only once, no matter which machines are required for production. From a client's perspective, conforming data to a mailing company's house format may appear to be easy, but it usually isn't.

Data Formats

Customers who send PC-based word processing or spreadsheet files should make sure that all their data components can be automatically parsed out. Although Word and Excel files may at first glance look like they're properly formatted, minor inconsistencies in line breaks, character spacing, and field positioning will require new programming code to be written. Most anomalies can be fixed and corrected, but this process is easiest for the mailing company because their data processing staff is using the same format. Instead of concentrating on who should do the data processing, a better approach is to focus on saving time and money, regardless of which company does the work. Again, good communication will determine the most cost-efficient and effective course of action.

TECH TIP If ASCII or database formats are used, once again software most likely will need to be written to find line and record breaks and prepare the data for postal presorts and address verification. While it's possible to put most lists in proper mailing condition, some hard-to-use files require a lot of programming time and subsequently cost a lot of money.

Data Manipulation

Splitting large files into smaller ones may reduce postal discounts. Assume you are mailing offers to prospective credit card applicants and are segmenting your database into four different categories of credit worthiness. If the job is processed in four lots instead of one, extra data processing will be required and postal discounts will decrease, unless the job is commingled prior to mail stream entry. If the components (envelope, letter, BRE, etc.) are the same for all four groups and the offer can be coded into specific fields, then the whole job should be processed and mailed in its entirety, saving a lot of postage.

On the other hand, if separate files are combined into one big file and field codes are stripped out, it will be difficult to appropriately match records and variable copy. If a mailing has physically different components (size, colors, shape, etc.)

and the combined data files no longer have unique field and record break indicators, matching the right record and offer may not be possible.

If the job is run multiple-up, the data must be processed in an appropriate order. "East/west" imaging (first name left, next name right, etc.) will cause problems because the stacks will be out of order after final trimming. Instead, "north/south" ordering allows jobs to be processed, separated, and married with the job ending up in proper mailing sequence. If a job is to be commingled, then the data needs to be sorted in straight zip code sequence. For mail that is to be drop-shipped but not commingled, processing needs to be done first by zip code order and second by destination SCF (section center facility) and BMC (bulk mail center). Bundle breaking is applicable when other auxiliary functions—such as match mailings—will be performed.

Presorting

Mailings need to be processed through USPS-approved CASS and CPC-approved address accuracy software to verify that addresses are in the proper format and are deliverable. After CASS certification, presort qualification software (i.e., Mail Stream or Group One) verifies postal discounts by tabulating mail counts in each zip code. When the process is complete, all records will have nine-digit zip codes and be in appropriate groups and sort order for efficient production, and all statistics required by the USPS will be generated.

Customers should discuss data preparation issues with their direct mail services provider prior to sending out jobs. Making corrections to large data files and electronically transmitting them at the last minute may cause production problems. Even if T1 lines are available, a five million record data file averaging 800 bytes per record still takes a long time to transmit. Without a T1 line, the transmission of large data files is highly impractical. In addition, your direct mailing services company still needs to get data to fit their format, and more likely than not, some programming will be necessary. Although this usually isn't difficult, invariably time is limited this late in the production process.

PAL POINT... There's a lot to consider when planning your next direct mail job. With the recent postal increase, it is more urgent than ever to squeeze out every cent of postal savings. Prevent production headaches by collaborating with your direct mail services provider early in the planning process. Working together, you should be able to develop a good data processing system that saves you time and money.

16

Mailing Lists

—with Adam Van Wye, Vice President, Mailing Lists, Inc.

There is little argument among direct mail experts that the mailing list constitutes the most vital component of a direct mail campaign. As attractive as an offer may be and as dynamic as the piece may look, these areas become inconsequential if the mailing is sent to the wrong audience.

The first step to consider when contemplating list selection is defining your target audience. Who are the most likely responders to the offer? If marketing to consumers, can you pinpoint certain demographics or psychographics (lifestyle characteristics) that seem to profile your likely customers? If you are a business-to-business marketer, do certain sized companies or industries make more sense than others? Are there geographic constraints? Ask yourself, "Where do my customers come from?" or, in the case of a new product or service, "What are the characteristics of my best prospects?"

Experienced mailing professionals know that analyzing core customer characteristics makes perfect sense. A formal way to accomplish this is to append customer and qualified prospect databases with business or consumer demographic data. There are less formal ways too—such as sending a brief survey to some of your best customers. In either case, it is important to understand as much as possible regarding your target audience because this will allow you to make intelligent list decisions, starting with the type of lists you purchase.

Two Classifications

The two general classifications of mailing lists are referred to as "compiled lists" and "response lists." Each is as it sounds. A compiled list is a grouping of common elements such as a list of all attorneys in a given area, for example. Compilers rely on public sources such as telephone books, directories, mortgage data, census data, annual reports, and trade publications to gather as much data on individuals and businesses as possible. On the other hand, response lists are comprised of responders to direct mail or other direct marketing solicitations. People and companies get placed on these lists because they buy, subscribe, attend, or donate.

All things being equal, response lists typically outperform compiled lists since these names represent proven buyers of similar services or goods. Purchasers of compiled lists have no idea if any of the names are inclined at all to respond to direct mail solicitations; in fact, many will likely never respond. Not surprisingly, response lists are more expensive than compiled lists, but are usually justified because of their higher response rates. There are also unique selections, such as "recency" (newer names on lists are better prospects than those who purchased long ago but haven't since) and "price points" (some lists allow name selection based on the dollar volume of past purchases), both of which help bolster response rates but are impractical for compiled lists.

Why bother with compiled lists? For starters, compiled lists are intended to provide as complete a universe of names as possible. Local merchants that cater to customers within a handful of zip codes would likely select compiled lists since a response list would probably yield very few names in a small geographic area. (Note: Many response lists have a 5,000-name minimum order.) A business-to-business mar-keter looking to reach all CEOs with 100+ employees in a given state wouldn't want just those that subscribe to a particular publication. In cases like this, marketers would be better served by purchasing compiled lists.

Selection criteria for compiled lists are too numerous to discuss in depth. Some of the more popular parameters for business lists include:

- Industry (often via SIC codes)
- Employee count
- Sales volume
- Job title or function

There are also specialized files such as brand-new businesses. Consumer selections include demographics such as:

- Age
- Estimated income
- Gender
- Presence of children
- Home ownership
- Length of residence
- Education level

There are also many specialized databases offering things such as:

- New movers
- New homeowners
- People with home equity loans or second mortgages
- Pre- and postnatal women

There are also more sophisticated models based on various pieces of data designed to predict specific consumer behavior.

Finally, there are self-reported lists, often derived from questionnaires, surveys, and product warranty cards. These lists rely on individuals completing information about themselves and their households and are regarded as being a bit more accurate than conventional compiled lists.

Once you're ready to embark upon list research, a good starting place is to contact your local Direct Marketing Association (DMA) affiliate to find a list broker. List brokers should be willing to do a lot of legwork for you and recommend lists to suit your needs. Good brokers will also lend a hand in trafficking orders as well as in assisting with the tracking and monitoring of responses.

Mailers who are inclined to research lists on their own should acquaint themselves with list compilers and/or list managers. There are several major list compilers of consumer and business lists, many of which may be identified over the Internet. Mailers interested in specific response or compiled lists can work directly with list managers or have their brokers do so. The list manager, unlike a list broker, is the exclusive sales and marketing agent for specific list property. Many list management companies represent a lot of lists, many within the same category or subject area. Therefore, they may have additional list recommendations for you to consider. List managers are responsible for advertising and promoting their managed lists as well as fulfilling count requests, clearing sample mail pieces, coordinating orders with respective service bureaus, and collecting list rental revenues on the list owner's behalf.

PAL POINT... Choose your lists carefully! It's wise to end where we began. You can design the best possible piece and take advantage of all the postal discounts in the world, but if you mail to the wrong recipients, you'll waste a heck of a lot of your precious promotional budget.

Data Cleansing

17

CHAPTER

Companies that manage your data manage your future success. Fully service your data needs by selecting a data management services company with a wealth of direct mail industry knowledge. Experienced data partners will help you avoid pitfalls and costly errors while allowing you to get a good night's sleep. After verifying your instructions and requirements, a good data house will:

• Ensure that your data files contain all required components, match the data file layout, and are otherwise error-free.

• Build cleansing processes in a logical manner to ensure accurate data output.

• Extract a representative record dump to test the cleansing processes prior to full production. This test will reduce the likelihood of logic errors and unnecessary multiple cleanup runs.

• Verify key fields such as state or province codes. For example, in the U.S., "MI" is frequently used in error for both Missouri and Mississippi, whiles it's really the state code for Michigan. Similarly, in Canada, "PQ" or "QU" are frequently used instead of the correct "QC."

• Check that apartment and suite numbers are located in a standardized position within an address field or are placed in a field of their own. Incorrect placement will reduce your project's chances for proper delivery.

• Ensure that proper recipient names are used. Up to 60% of the general population prefers to be addressed by a different salutation than the one used on most of their mail. Using a separate salutation field instead of a parsed first name field may boost your response rate. Properly place and punctuate name components such as honorific, first name, middle initial, last name, and suffix. Initial names like "J.R. Ewing" often are truncated to "Dear J" unless a separate salutation field is used.

• Develop and update your house lists. Use a salutation field. Verify that each record has properly spelled name components (Claire, Clair, Clare), gender codes (Pat, Francis, Robin), casing (DeLane, Delane, deLane), and punctuation (L'Argent, Largent).

Merge/Purge

The de-duping process removes duplicate records from single or multiple data files. Before beginning merge/purge or any other type of data manipulation, it is critically important that you understand exactly what the client expects as output before giving instructions to your data processing department.

There are three levels of merge/purge for consumer files: resident, household, or individual. (Business-to-business lists require a different process.) Be sure to double-check with your customer to determine what kind of list is being processed.

Resident level. This level of de-duplication removes all but one record from each address. For example, if John Doe and Mary Doe are each listed at 123 Main St. in separate records, only the first record will survive, while the other is dropped as a duplicate. The end result is that only one record will be mailed, which has an obvious associated cost saving.

Household level. This level removes all but one record with the same last name from each address. For example, if John Doe, Mary Doe, Sue Brown, and Joe Green all live at the same address, a household level de-duplication process will keep one of the Does, Sue Brown, and Joe Green. If John Doe appears in the data file first, Mary Doe will be dropped.

Individual level. This level will only remove duplicates with the same complete name from each address. For example, if John Doe, Mary Doe, Sue Brown, and Joe Green all live at the same address, an individual de-duplication will keep all of the records since each one is a different person.

Additional Data Files

Suppression/purge. Often clients request that certain people and/or households not receive mail. These types of requests, commonly referred to as "kill" files, can be made for many reasons. Two examples could be that they're employees of the competition or they've asked to be removed from your mailing list. In order to accommodate these types of requests, a customer-supplied "suppression" (or "purge") file needs to be supplied. When records on the merge/purge file match records on the suppression file, they're immediately dropped.

List priority. Some customers will furnish a "priority listing." This list will show which files take priority over other files when it comes to dropping duplicate records. This means that when duplicate records are found, the list with the highest priority loses the least amount of duplicate records because the duplicates are dropped from the lower priority files first. For example, if a customer supplies a "house" database file of customers as well as several rental files, the customer database will have the highest priority. The rental lists can then be ranked based upon rental costs. For example, assuming your most costly lists are more accurate, you'd probably want to assign a higher priority to the expensive lists and less priority to cheaper lists.

Weighted-Value Merge/Purge

What happens when data files contain the same individual, but there's a misspelling? Would two pieces of mail be sent to John Doe and Jon Doe at the same address? If an individual merge/purge "match code" process were used, the answer would be "yes." (Match code merge/purges cannot compensate for key field character variation and will result in what is known as an "underkill.")

The solution to this vexing data problem is to perform a "weighted-value" merge/purge, whereby you determine which fields and record lengths are most appropriate for your project. Sophisticated weighted-value merge/purge algorithms enable you to avoid variances within name and address components and reduce your overkill/underkill error frequency. For example, a properly constructed weighted-value merge/purge program will detect three variants of the following "Mike Keenan" records and eliminate two.

1. Mike Keenan, 201 Carlaw Ave., Toronto, ON, (416) 461-9271

2. Michael Kennan, 201 Carlow Ave., Toronto, ON, (416) 461-9201

3. M. Kenan, 201 Carlaw Rd., Toronto, ON, (416) 461-9271

Most merge/purges are based upon data files being sorted first by postal code in ascending sequence. Grouping records together by running an address

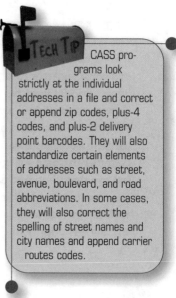

Tech Tip

CASS programs look strictly at the individual addresses in a file and correct or append zip codes, plus-4 codes, and plus-2 delivery point barcodes. They will also standardize certain elements of addresses such as street, avenue, boulevard, and road abbreviations. In some cases, they will also correct the spelling of street names and city names and append carrier routes codes.

verification/correction program prior to merge/purge is usually recommended.

CASS Certification

Running data through a CASS (Coding Accuracy Support System) certification process "scrubs" data records to make them as deliverable as possible. The USPS establishes the standards for data cleanliness.

All of these elements help make mail records more deliverable. Depending on the material being mailed and the mail class used, the USPS will require that this list hygiene process be run every ninety days.

NCOA

The NCOA (National Change of Address) program is directed by the USPS and licensed to only a few vendors throughout the United States. Make sure you choose a mailing services provider with a USPS license to perform NCOA.

NCOA uses the change of address cards individuals and businesses submit to the USPS when they move. This move data is kept for a rolling thirty-six months and is updated every two weeks. Your customer files are matched against this "move" database. If a match is found, the new information is appended to the record. Only mailers can legally use this process; it cannot be used for any other purpose.

The USPS strictly enforces NCOA rules. One pertinent rule is that a signed order acknowledgment must be on file before a job can be processed.

PAL POINT... Data cleansing is a vitally important activity and often makes a critical difference in terms of mailing deliverability, response rates, and profitability. For more detailed information on merge/purge, see Appendices 6 and 7.

CHAPTER 18

Palletization

Have you ever wondered how your direct mail production services company manages to get your high-volume mailing jobs into the mail stream right and on time? To be successful, they probably break these types of jobs into smaller, more manageable units, which allows them to more easily keep track of the shear volume of data, paper, and materials involved. What manufacturing process makes this possible? In a word: palletization.

Palletization techniques enable high-volume jobs to become "modular," thereby allowing production workers to make sure that each pallet of mail is properly processed and shipped. By running palletization software, high-volume direct mailers can work on less intimidating quantities, one pallet at a time. All of a sudden, manufacturing, quality control, and drop shipping become much easier, production errors decrease, and accountability increases.

Consider a hypothetical million-piece mailing. After your data presorts are completed, your job might be broken into 100 pallets averaging 10,000 pieces each. Since each pallet is sequentially numbered, a production manager now has the ability to control all letter-shop processes—i.e., laser imaging, converting, folding, bindery, and inserting—pallet by pallet. What just has been accomplished? You've taken an unwieldy million-piece job and broken it down into very manageable smaller-sized jobs.

TECH TIP Palletization simplifies staging issues during and after production. Designing floor staging and trucking plans for work-in-process and/or finished goods is fast and easy. Since every pallet is already sequentially numbered, all your mailer has to do is make sure that pallets 1–24 are loaded into staging area A, 25–48 in staging area B and so forth.

In addition, there are tracking benefits associated with palletization too. When working on large jobs, it's difficult to ensure that every required process happens to every piece of mail. What if the response to your mailing from the Mobile, Alabama, area falls short of expectations? While there are many possible causes for this result, three of the more obvious include:

- The offer didn't appeal to people in Mobile (strategy problem).
- The design and/or copy didn't appeal to people in Mobile (design/copy problem).
- Less mail arrived at destination in Mobile than other parts of the country (production problem).

An obvious first step is to rule out production problems as being the source of your low response rate. To do this, examine your palletization records and verify that your mail destined for Mobile was properly produced and sent. If you discover it was, production error can be eliminated. Then you can confidently begin a core analysis of the project's strategy and design.

PAL POINT... Palletization is one of those behind-the-scenes processes that direct mailing professionals should know about. There will come a time in the careers of aspiring industry executives when their knowledge of issues like this get a troubled job out right and on time. Efficient production depends on good project planning and execution. As always, get advice from your direct mailing services company early in the job design phase.

Nth Criteria Select

19

What happens when you wish to send a mailing to only a portion of your database? There are many reasons why you may need to do this. Budgeting, test marketing, and target marketing all come to mind.

Let's say you have 100,000 mailing records in your database and for budget reasons can only afford to send 80,000 pieces. In this case, don't send mail to the first 80,000 people and skip the rest. Doing so may result in your skipping California, for instance, and would badly skew the results. A better way to proceed would be to select eight out of every ten records—in this case, sequentially by zip code— via an "Nth criteria select" process. If your mailing house deselects every fifth and tenth record, your mailing size will end up at the desired 80,000 pieces, and each zip code will be proportionately reduced.

Nth criteria select needn't only be done by geography. Perhaps you're working on a high-cost/high-profile piece that targets large charitable donors. Due to this project's parameters, you will need your average donation size to be larger than usual to justify the cost of the promotion. It may make sense to target people and organizations with histories of donating large amounts in the past. If so, go into your field with previous donation historical data and select only

	A	B	C	D	E	F
1	Abbott	John	123 Main St.	Hometown	PA	1523
2	Abel	Rosalee	2072 Broadway Ave.	Hometown	PA	1523
3	Abernathy	Theodore	1181 W. Chester Rd.	Hometown	PA	1523
4	Abrams	Christopher	2021 Walnut Ave.	Hometown	PA	1523
5	Adair	Ronald	1185 W. Chester Rd.	Hometown	PA	1523
6	Adams	Roberta	423 Main St.	Hometown	PA	1523
7	Adamson	George	659 May St.	Hometown	PA	1523
8	Adkins	Cynthia	845 Roberts Rd.	Hometown	PA	1523
9	Agnew	Tracey	601 Spruce St.	Hometown	PA	1523
10	Aiken	David	679 Oak Ave.	Hometown	PA	1523
11	Albert	Herbert	601 E. May St.	Hometown	PA	1523
12	Alcorn	Stanley	2092 Lloy Ave.	Hometown	PA	1523
13	Aldrich	Louis	642 Abstract Way	Hometown	PA	1523
14	Alexander	Robert	1137 Aliquippa Ave.	Hometown	PA	1523
15	Alfred	William	832 Liberty St.	Hometown	PA	1523
16	Allan	Alvin	917 Washington Blvd.	Hometown	PA	1523
17	Allen	Julia	801 Smith Lane	Hometown	PA	1523

Sheet1 / Sheet2 / Sheet3 /

those records that meet or exceed a certain threshold of giving.

Nth Criteria Select Examples

Example 1. Harte-Hanks Baltimore, the company of one of the authors, has a corporate client that manufactures fine china. Whenever certain china patterns are about to go on sale, the client asks Harte-Hanks to identify households in their database that have bought the same patterns in the past and send a highly targeted mailing just to those people. Also, this same company regularly tries to give a few stores at a time a sales boost by sending promotional mailings to people who have shopped in these stores before.

Example 2. Harte-Hanks Baltimore also does a lot of work within the financial community and sends out many promotional mailings from financial institutions. Nth criteria select methods allow clients to choose recipients based on desired credit scores and make different offers to different people based on credit worthiness. For example, your good credit may get you a pre-approved credit card with a low rate while your next-door neighbor may get an offer for a secured card at 21% interest.

PAL POINT... Like so much else in direct mail, it's the little things that count. The Nth criteria select process helps mailing professionals meet their budget constraints while properly targeting their best prospects.

20

ULTIMATE DATA PAL

Building Data Tables

Here's an attractive goal: Reduce data entry and computing processing time while increasing accuracy. How? Build "tables" into your database.

Consider Harte-Hanks Baltimore's china manufacturing client again. If the data entry staff must type "bone white," "forest green," or "Antarctica white" into the color field, you can be certain that there would be many misspellings. If specific offers for more china were dependent on getting the color right, wouldn't it be more efficient to assign a number to this particular field in each record? Of course it would. Typing "3" or "ant" instead of "Antarctica white" is a lot faster and far less subject to data entry errors. Then, when your mailing house processes the mail, the field entry would be cross-referenced to the data table with the china patterns, and "Antarctica white" would be printed properly in the body of the letter.

Another Harte-Hanks Baltimore customer—this time a vehicle manufacturing company—periodically sends different promotional offers to its customers. This client believes in local control and subsequently pushes some marketing decisions down to the decision chain. Dealers choose which promotions to offer—such as $20 off a lube job, free wipers, car wash, etc. In addition to being variable (i.e., discount amount), these offers are referenced in different tables so dealers can easily choose multiple promotions if they wish. If so, all they have to do is say to their

TECH TIP In addition, data tables reduce computer-processing time because each record contains fewer bytes. Although today's computing technology has vastly improved, smaller files still mean faster data processing and transmission times. This is especially true if limited bandwidth data communications lines are involved.

supplier, "For my mailing, we want promos 1, 4, 8, and 13 mailed sequentially (via Nth criteria select of course) to my database." And that is exactly what they'd get.

Address and Barcode Standards

There are innumerable ways that mailings can go awry. In order to comply with USPS rules and achieve maximum postal discounts, many rules need to be followed. Although there are no substitutes for the *USPS Domestic Mail Manual* (DMM) or *International Mail Manual* (IMM), let's first briefly consider the basics of POSTNET barcodes.

Direct mailers receive discounts for mailings with POST-NET (Postal Numeric Encoding Technique) barcodes because they allow the USPS to process the

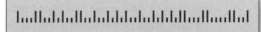

mail more efficiently on highly automated equipment. These barcodes are graphic representations of the five-digit-plus-four zip code, the two-digit delivery point code, and a "check" digit code.

To make the system work for everyone, the USPS requires mail to adhere to certain deliverability standards. This is why mailing lists must be processed through USPS-approved CASS (Coding Accuracy Support System) and PAVE (Presort Accuracy Validation Evaluation) software.

There are many reasons why direct mailers should prioritize using as clean a list as possible:

- Less mail rejected when processed with USPS-approved software
- Higher percentage of deliverable mail
- Less mail is sent at higher-cost "residual" rates
- Fewer duplicates are sent to the same address
- Fewer "underkills" (when mail is not sent to a desired address)

• Mail arrives at intended destinations faster

In addition, mail must adhere to postal regulations regarding shape, size, weight, color, and image positioning.

Address Insert Shift Test

Sometimes the simplest tests are best. To ensure that the printed address on an insert shows through the window, all you have to do is:

- Tap the mail piece separately on its left and right edges to jog the insert as far to the left and right as it can go.

- As each side is tapped, check that a clear space of at least ⅛ in. (3 mm) is still maintained between the left and right edges of the address and the left and right window edges.

- Do the same for the top and bottom edges as well.

PAL POINT... Like baseball, direct mail is a game of inches ...and ounces. Pay attention to the little things because you will save money and your job. Be safe and frequently consult with your best friend: the DMM.

CHAPTER 22

PDF Workflow

—with Art Simpson, Vice President, EU Services

The printing and direct mail industries continue to evolve from the arcane method of stripping film. New technologies that turn electronic art files into beautifully printed pieces are improving almost daily, or so it seems. But with greater features comes greater complexity. How do you keep up with the changes? Well, the answer can be found in just three letters: PDF.

PDF, or Portable Document Format, is almost everywhere. Perhaps you've downloaded a PDF file as a convenient way to print tax forms from the IRS website. Well, PDF technology works wonders in ink-on-paper environments as well. PDFs are an essential part of a digital workflow system that gets jobs out quickly, accurately, and with greater flexibility.

The key to the flexibility of a PDF workflow is that a single PDF file contains all the information necessary to see a job through its entire life cycle, not just during the printing process itself. The same file that's used to create the printed piece can be viewed online as a proof. (Note: It's also the same file that EU Services uses in an online inventory system, allowing quick access to a visual "snapshot" of every piece we've produced, whether that was last year or last week.)

The accuracy of a PDF file is unparalleled, since every aspect of a document to be printed is included in the file—most importantly, images and fonts. In a PDF file, the fonts are actually written into the file's code. So there's no more hunting for fonts or seeing the wrong font make its way onto a proof! With a PDF-based workflow, a lot of time-consuming prepress tasks are eliminated.

Online Proofing

The capabilities of the PDF format as a proofing method are nearly limitless. Again, there simply is no comparison between a PDF-based proofing system and most traditional proofing methods in terms of speed. In some cases, "proofing" used to mean actually printing a sample piece for the client, right on a press. Sure, it looked great, but it took forever to do. And changes? These could tack hours onto the job.

The PDF workflow system improves on the past tremendously by allowing proofing to be done online, in full color on a computer monitor. The same file that will actually be used to print the job is available via email or on the Web as soon as it's ready for proofing. This "instant 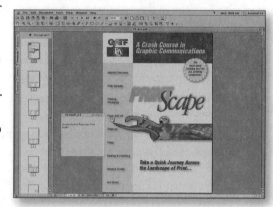 access" shaves off a great deal of valuable time for direct mailers either printing or outsourcing project components, because it allows them to immediately make changes to the proof.

Another key benefit to viewing proofs online is that multiple parties can see the same file simultaneously. If two decision-makers can't be in the same office, building, or even the same area code, they can both view and make changes to the PDF file. Currently, this is accomplished via email. However, there soon should be an interface that will allow several users to collaborate at a single website, making changes in real time and seeing those changes immediately noted in the image onscreen.

Don't mistake online PDF proofs as just a "quick and dirty" tool for monitoring the progress of a job. Many project managers appreciate the efficiency of PDF proofs so much that they make final approvals based on them. Though the color onscreen is not exactly as it will appear on the printed piece, most clients feel it's close enough and don't need to see an actual hardcopy color proof, unless it's a color-critical job. Of course, a good rapport between printer and client is essential for PDF proofs to be the sole proofing method.

Online Inventory System

One of the greatest advantages of PDF's flexibility is its use in a digital inventory system. With a typical inventory system, a scan must be made of every job document for a customer to view it digitally. These scans are then converted into TIFF files and posted online somewhere. This is a cumbersome process at best, and offers no flexibility if a piece needs to be changed or updated.

It's a different story with PDFs. The file that was used to print a piece is also used in a PDF-based inventory system that's accessible via the Web. Does your customer want another print run but lack a physical sample of the job? No problem—as long as inventoried components in PDF formats are available online. They would just access their individual password-protected area of the website and place a reorder. This is a much quicker and simpler solution than looking through piles of old printed samples.

Fulfillment and mailing are growing businesses. There's a lot of information that a fulfillment department needs in conjunction with a printed piece that, on older systems, can be quite difficult to coordinate. But using a PDF-based workflow helps contain and manage all of this information. As a job moves through the system, the same file travels with it, allowing everyone involved with a project to actually "see" it along the way.

PAL POINT... Although implementing PDF-based job and inventory management systems can appear complex, trust your comprehensive direct mail services provider to guide the process of developing a faster and more accurate workflow.

100% Mailings

There are occasions when a mailing client needs all addresses on their database to be sent by mail...guaranteed. If your job involves invoices, account statements, proxies, annual reports, etc., you need 100% deliverability. (This is in contrast to many promotional mailings where some spoilage is acceptable.) If you've been through this process before, you probably understand some of the basic complexities of what is known in the industry as "100% mailings." The golden rule in producing 100% mailings is to plan for this at the beginning of a job.

To comply with this requirement, your mailing services company must alter its standard operating procedures to maneuver around an unavoidable manufacturing reality: production spoilage. Manufacturing processes must be implemented that ensure the recapture of all pieces spoiled during production. Then these pieces need to be identified, matched against the master database, and produced again in a follow-up production run.

A company of one of the authors advises its customers with 100% mailing requirements to design an area somewhere on their piece where a unique barcode can be imaged. After the first production run, they gather all spoilage and scan every piece, giving an electronic record locator that shows which addresses need to be recreated. Next, the scanned results are downloaded and matched against the original database to create a new data file. Then the previously spoiled pieces (twice—just in case we spoil the spoil) are re-imaged, thereby producing a new mailing that plugs the gaps of the first and returning the desired result: a 100% mailing.

In the event that your client won't allow you to image a barcode anywhere on the piece, the process of matching spoilage to the master database becomes more time-consuming. When barcodes are objectionable, try to convince the decision-maker to at least let you print a unique sequence number (a type of record locator) inconspicuously placed somewhere on the piece. If you can, recreating the data file only involves the additional step of re-keying a short string of text characters from each spoiled piece, thus enabling the computer to identify the addresses for re-imaging. While re-keying sequence numbers is less efficient and precise than barcode scanning, it sure beats the last alternative: manual re-keying of field data.

In general, plan to add an additional 10% to the cost of production, more or less depending on project complexity and the number of manufacturing operations involved. If the project is straightforward, such as laser imaging, converting, and inserting, your mailing services provider should anticipate minimal spoilage, and your price premium should be somewhere near 10%. However, if your job involves a lot of additional bindery or other manufacturing operations, there will be more spoilage, and this premium percentage will increase, perhaps to 20%.

PAL POINT... 100% mailings require extra planning, materials, machine makereadies, and production time. It should be no surprise that 100% mailings cost more to produce.

Postcard Programs

*—with Sylvia Konkel, Vice President of Marketing,
EU Services*

If you're looking for a proven, low-cost direct-response marketing vehicle, consider the timeless, versatile, and, yes, safe postcard. Compared to other types of printed promotions, postcard campaigns are relatively inexpensive to produce. They deserve extra consideration, especially when timeliness and cost considerations are paramount.

Production and Postal Issues

A few areas can be "hot spots" when developing postcard mailings—all of which can be addressed in advance with good planning:

- **Size.** To qualify for postcard rates, pieces must be between 4¼×6 in. (108×152 mm) and 3½×5 in. (89×127 mm). Anything larger will mail at letter-size mail rates.

- **Paper thickness.** Most designers know that 7-pt. high bulk is the minimum postcard thickness. However, even

though this weight of paper meets USPS standards, it often has a flimsy feel to it. Consider increasing your paper thickness to 9-pt. or even higher.

- **Double postcards.** Folded postcards with perforated BRCs qualify for postcard postal rates, if the attached card is a true BRC. This means the second panel of the card must be detachable and mailable as a reply device. Don't add a folded panel just because you're running out of visual real estate. Otherwise, you'll end up with a rude postage surprise. The address side of the reply card must be folded inward. Also, the two panels must be sealed with one seal at either the top or the bottom.

• **Reflectance and barcode clear zones.** All USPS reflectance and barcode requirements apply to postcards.

• **Multiple versions.** If you're planning a multi-postcard campaign or printing similar versions together, specifying all the jobs to run together could save both time and money. Ganged production runs are just one area for potential savings. Also consider plate changes for simple text differences and hone-offs to accommodate multiple pre-printed codes.

Postcard Design: A Case Study

EU Services recently changed phone systems. As a result, hundreds of EU's employees were assigned new direct dial extensions, and word of this change had to be communicated to customers and vendors quickly. Direct mail, broadcast fax, broadcast email, and word of mouth through the sales and service team were considered. EU's marketing department felt that a postcard mailing targeted to all customers, vendors, and industry friends would be the best channel to reach everyone as quickly and directly as possible.

Information from EU's Customer Advisory Board was incorporated in designing the card itself. Deb Tompkins, EU customer advisory member and sales manager for JAM Communications in Washington, D.C., provided the following insights:

> *"Postcards can solve company-specific marketing problems. Don't struggle with the endless search for the 'perfect' image, because it rarely exists. Instead, consider creating original artwork. Since*

the physical aspects of postcards are limited, they cry out for creative, jazzy, and unusual designs. Get my attention with the artwork. Then keep the copy brief and simple, but personalize it whenever possible."

PAL PoiNT... If you're looking for a different way to get your message to your marketplace, or if you have budget constraints, consider a postcard program. Postcards aren't just for vacation pictures anymore.

CHAPTER

Label Programs

Labels are a great way for both nonprofit organizations and for-profit companies to achieve great direct mail results. Many direct mailers have pigeonholed label programs as effective, but infrequent, seasonal events. There are two problems with this approach. First, direct mailers are missing out on good opportunities with a proven marketing vehicle. Second, program managers don't learn how to efficiently purchase and administer them.

There are a lot of companies and organizations that only think of direct mail label programs for the winter holiday season. This is outdated thinking. Many label jobs now have mail drop dates in the late winter, spring, and summer. Labels aren't just for Christmas anymore.

Mailing professionals who buy a lot of the same direct mail components become skilled at squeezing good results out of small investments. However, infrequent purchases don't attract the same scrutiny as other programs and tend not

be bought as efficiently. Opting for the "easy" purchase route may cost you more than you realize. Let's examine why labels are effective as promotional items.

Labels Work

Today's specialty landscape is full of promotional products. Direct mail label programs have endured because recipients get a useful product that can be used every day and proudly displays their affinity with a desirable organization. As a result, the target audience is likely to respond favorably to the solicitation request. Historically, nonprofit organizations have been the main users of label programs because their target audiences appreciate the functionality of the labels themselves and are eager to display their affinity with the soliciting organization.

Labels are desirable premiums because (1) production can be highly automated and (2) final product can be easily delivered through the USPS. Many competing specialty products such as pens, small calendars, and coffee cups can't be manufactured as easily and cost more to mail without necessarily producing better response rates. Sheets of labels can be designed as just another insert in a direct mail package. Since they are so automation friendly, labels are very appropriate for high-volume mailings.

Labels Work in the For-Profit Arena Too

Although nonprofits have been the traditional users of direct mail label programs, for-profit companies have discovered ways of hopping on the bandwagon. For example, some financial institutions advise their customers to attach labels imprinted with theft protection information to their credit cards before initial use. If a consumer's cards have "protection" labels affixed to them and are stolen, the theory is that thieves will be deterred from using them. Nonfinancial sector companies have sent labels to their customers for use on windshields, phones, and membership cards. Labels are an inexpensive way to disburse useful information in bite-sized doses.

Design Flexibility

Direct mail labels can follow traditional formats, or may be designed to be as unique as fingerprints. The following features can be added or changed to meet your special marketing needs:

- Size of the sheet
- Number of ink colors
- Foil stamping
- Size and position of folds and panels
- Label paper stock and color
- Intricate diecuts
- Label size and shape
- Number of labels per sheet and per recipient
- Graphics
- Sheet orientation (landscape/portrait)

Design options are unlimited. When designing your label sheet, allow a margin for pin-feed holes on each side of the paper. Some label manufacturers can print, foil stamp, diecut, and strip away waste inline before imprinting, inserting, and drop shipping or mailing. If you're straying from standard label formats, get advice early in the design process because some designs can't have waste automatically stripped, which dramatically increases costs.

Don't forget about mailing discounts. Since labels can be inserted just like any other mailing component, you can benefit from most postal savings programs. For example, commingling and drop shipping together can save prudent label direct mailers up to $47 per thousand pieces in postal discounts.

Technology's Role

Historically, label companies have relied on 16-in. (406-mm) web presses for production, but now larger web sizes are more common, saving a lot of money because of multiple-up layout flexibility. Also, high-speed, high-quality, eight-color printing plus inline foil stamping (or nine-color printing without foil stamping) is a reality in many parts of the country. In addition, the quality of high-speed, 300-dpi continuous laser printing is superb. Rapidly advancing technology has spurred the formation of strategic alliances between label printers and direct mailers, giving their mutual customers better access to one-stop solutions.

According to Tim Roberts, president of ROI Technologies, foil stamping has been shown to increase label program response rates by at least 1%. Since foil can now be applied at speeds in excess of 225 feet per minute (19,000 8½-in. cutoffs per hour), foil is no longer cost-prohibitive. If cost reduction is a top goal, you may be able to use magnetic dies instead of hard metal ones, saving up to 80%. Faster production and more bells and whistles aren't free. For example, high-speed inline web diecutting tolerances are less than forgiving. Properly produced labels require "kiss" cuts, which must be within 0.0025 in. (0.06 mm) accuracy, so the labels peel away cleanly from the carrier sheet.

Buying Expertise

Direct mail professionals have a lot of options when purchasing label programs. As mentioned earlier, most people don't buy label programs often, and this may result in comparatively low levels of buying expertise. Outsourcing direct mail label programs to "professional fundraising companies" is attractive to some people because it's easy. In exchange for a healthy portion of the net proceeds, a professional fundraising company will handle the entire program for a client—soup to nuts. Essentially, all a nonprofit administrator has to do is hand off a mailing list, wait a few months, and receive a check for a portion of the funds raised.

However, if a nonprofit wishes to maximize net revenue, it should consider buying the label program direct. In exchange for a little more hands-on management, a non-profit can significantly increase its fundraising net revenues. For example, if a label program costs $50,000 to produce and administer and generates $100,000 of funds, the contribution margin is $50,000. If a professional fundraiser is involved, this $50,000 will be split somehow between the fundraising company and the nonprofit. Professional management companies may not take advantage of the latest manufacturing technology, and since the client has little direct involvement, production and administrative costs tend to be very high. A scenario in which the nonprofit receives less than half of the normal net proceeds (in this case, $25,000) is certainly possible.

Label program managers in this situation should ask the question: "Does the ease of working with a professional fundraiser offset the loss of $25,000?" Some will say yes and others no, depending on their circumstances.

PAL POINT... Label programs work because they shout, "I'm a member." This is good for both the label giver and the end user because they enter a symbiotic relationship whereby both parties benefit. Encourage your customers to buy direct mail label programs smarter and more frequently.

SECTION 3
Direct Mail Production

Letter Text and Variable Imaging

One of the certainties of direct mail is that the pace of the industry keeps on quickening. Even though mailings are more complex than ever, turnaround times nonetheless are becoming shorter. From a copywriter and designer's point of view, waiting until the last minute can be beneficial because the latest and most relevant information can be added. However, delay has negative consequences that ripple throughout the production process.

Let's consider how compressed schedules affect letter text and variable image positioning. In the not-too-distant past, simple text files were converted into laser formats that were limited at best, which easily allowed text to be "dropped in" at the last moment. Even though today's sophisticated "publishing" tools have made incredible gains in the world of personalization, on the data preparation side, there are now more ways than ever for something to go wrong. The bottom line is this: Try to give your mailing services provider enough time so it can confidently prepare your job and meet your scheduling needs.

Expectations

At a minimum, data preparation and mail service providers should be able to accept text formatted as word processing documents, thereby retaining most properties intended by the designer and marketer. It is even better if graphic layout program files, such as QuarkXPress, can be accepted. If so, the actual designer's file can be used, complete with variable and static text and graphic images.

When your direct mail service provider laser-images your variable copy on either cut-sheet or continuous forms, there are many things it must be aware of to prevent costly production errors.

Matt Copy

When a personalized letter, reply, or document is part of the job, make sure decision-makers see and approve a "matt copy," which is the part of the letter, reply, or document that will be "pre-printed" prior to shipping the form to your mail services provider for customization. This helps ensure that personalization, variable laser imaging, and pre-printing all match in typeface, size, and style.

Tech Tip

It's best if clients provide this "matt copy" in electronic form in an acceptable format. Once the mailing services provider's data processing department has set the matt copy, the "proof" should be read for typographical, spelling, punctuation, spacing, and any other kinds of errors.

Whitepaper Proofs

Prior to live laser signoffs, "whitepaper" proofs (laser-imaged proofs on plain paper) should be created so only that which is to be laser-imaged is clearly seen. Again, as with matt copy, the entire document must be proofed, word for word, graphic by graphic. Look for items such as:

- Spacing between words
- Spacing between lines
- Placement of name and address block
- Codes (check number of digits, alpha/numeric, starting digit, etc.)

Be certain that the approved matt copy and the laser-printed text and images agree.

Live Laser Proofs

Once the whitepaper signoffs have been approved and all data file processing is complete, the mailing services com-pany should offer "live" laser signoffs for final approval. Again, verify accuracy of copy, text, and window positioning before beginning the production run. Both the client and the account manager must verify the proof for accuracy.

Lastly, be wary of pushing the variable personalization envelope beyond the integrity of your data. For example, sending a personalized solicitation expounding the female benefits of a health club to a male named "Pat" will do more harm than good.

PAL PoiNT... Do not rush through the seemingly tedious proofing process. Find a quiet spot, go through the file, concentrate on that specific job, and then begin proofing. Take your time, because this is where a lot of mistakes happen. Try not to compress turnaround times beyond the turnaround guidelines preferred by your direct mail services provider. Although it may be possible to occasionally shorten delivery dates, the chances of error do increase.

27

Levels of Personalization

Personalization can range from "Dear Occupant" to a handwritten letter to anything in between. Due to superior speed and quality, laser imaging is now the most popular method of addressing and personalizing direct mail forms. Over the last decade, technological improvements have enabled the direct mail industry to leap forward in terms of personalization capabilities. Here are descriptions of the three basic levels of laser image personalization.

Basic Imaging

In its simplest form, laser imaging uses laser toner application technology to apply generic text and variable address information. In addition to the name and address block, a few words may also be variable depending on data fields containing geographic, sociographic, segmentation, or demographic criteria. Basic imaging personalization became prevalent during the early part of the 1990s.

Although many millions of pieces are still mailed with this level of laser imaging, it now fulfills only the lowest consumer expectation requirements. In order to provide the recipient with a more relevant message, direct marketers should consider stepping up their personalization effort.

Variable Imaging

Variable imaging adds more personalization and customization capabilities than basic imaging. In addition to imaging basic information such as recipient's name, address, and salutation, variable imaging allows marketers to insert and subtract sentences and even paragraphs depending on whether or not database "triggers" are activated. For example, if a person's name was acquired from a list of outdoor magazine subscribers, a specific reference may be made to either the publication or an outdoor lifestyle. If the next recipient's name was purchased from a cooking magazine list, the customized information could easily change from an outdoor to a cooking reference. Variable imaging means that recipients receive information and images that are more likely to appeal to them based on captured database information.

Variable Publishing

The highest level of personalization is "variable publishing." A true variably published document contains completely variable information from beginning to end. All images and text are specifically chosen for each recipient based on likely personal preferences. In addition to the content being completely variable, so is the layout. Consider a variably published newsletter. Not only are the text and images different throughout one production run, but so are the fonts, font sizes, number of columns, and even the masthead.

As long as the database has enough pertinent and accurate information to drive a variable publishing effort—this should be your first consideration—the final product can be an extremely meaningful piece of communication without resorting to low-value-added personalization efforts such as slapping the recipient's name everywhere.

PAL POINT... Personalization has come a long way in the past decade. In the early days, it took an effort just to get the recipient's name at the beginning of a paragraph and have the rest of the paragraph wrap properly. With higher-level variable imaging and variable publishing, the old days are long gone.

Continuous Laser Imaging

28

Is your large-volume direct mail project appropriate for continuous laser-imaging equipment? Have you dodged this technology because of image quality concerns? Rest assured that today's exciting high-speed machines are appropriate for many of the finest long-run direct mail projects.

Continuous laser imaging is great for a wide range of high-volume direct mail projects, including letters, order forms, statements, invoices, subscriptions, and self-mailers. Industries as diverse as financial services, the nonprofit sector, business-to-business, and consumer products have had great success with this technology.

Reasonable Expectations

Are you concerned that continuous laser imaging machines don't have the resolution you need? Think again. Admittedly, some companies still use equipment with low-end resolution, but most have moved to 300 dpi, 600 dpi, or even higher. With the growing availability of high-speed machines, there is no reason to settle for less. Direct mail designers have a wide array of fonts to choose from because many companies are heavily invested in this vital area.

Higher printing resolutions mean your scanned logos, signatures, and halftones will look great. Because of incredibly low data storage costs, there aren't any significant limitations on the size of graphic images. In the rare case that a large image is unwieldy, your data processing professional can split and remarry it before generating output. Toner registration to offset-printed forms is "dead-on" because continuous laser-imaging machines have accurate pin registration systems. (Occasionally, offset printing will move, but good laser imaging companies will attempt to "chase" the printing.)

Most equipment will accommodate two-up 8½×11-in. (216×279-mm) letters. Since rolls of paper or fan-folded forms are used by continuous laser imaging machinery, the length of a form is theoretically infinite, although cutoffs typically range between 3 and 24 in. (76 and 610 mm). For large-volume jobs, you will save time and money if your laser-imaging partner has roll-to-roll equipment because it's faster and less costly than fan-folded or cut-sheet production.

Design/Layout Tips

When working with large solid areas of toner coverage, direct mail designers should ask for technical advice before committing to a design. Today's machinery can lay down rich 100% toner coverage for a while, but as the run length increases, consistent quality depends on how the solid areas are positioned on the form. In general, large solids running parallel (horizontal) to the perforations are okay, but those running perpendicular (vertical) aren't.

Bad layouts may result in "toner starvation," which results in inconsistent and sometimes splotchy coverage. Be safe, and get advice from your data processing professional before signing off on risky and untested designs.

A common problem occurs when fan-folded stock is used and designers place copy too close to the perforations. Perforations form peaks and valleys as they pass over the drum, preventing toner from being applied properly. Combat this problem by position-

Tech Tip Once you've selected the right paper, make sure your offset printer uses heat-resistant, "laser-safe" inks. Forms that pass though high-speed continuous laser imaging equipment are exposed to high heat that will melt any and all wax present. Think of it this way: You wouldn't expect a candle to retain its shape in an oven. Don't expect the impossible from wax-based ink.

ing copy at least ½ in. (13 mm) away from all fan-folded (horizontal) perforations.

Paper and Ink

The paper you choose is important. Gloss-coated stock is almost impossible to run on continuous laser imaging equipment because toner cannot penetrate it, much less adhere. Fortunately, there are special stocks with glossy appearances that are porous enough to accept toner. Instead of naming specific enamel sheets, ask your mailing partner how the intended appearance can be achieved. Your mailing services company will try to help you get the look you want, decrease waste, increase productivity, meet deadlines, and lower mailing costs.

Diecut Forms

Direct mail jobs with diecuts can be eye-popping and beautiful, yet still run efficiently. However, there are a few caveats. Not only must diecut forms run well in high-speed imaging equipment, they also have to be compatible with other downstream machinery. Corners, edges, and other protruding points can cause problems on feeding units, saddle stitchers, inserters, commingling equipment, etc.

Kiss-cut jobs can be tricky. If the cuts are too deep, the carrier substrate may catch, resulting in frequent jams. If the cuts are too shallow, the labels won't peel off as intended, rendering the product functionally useless. SMR/Tytrek once converted a two-million-piece kiss-cut job. The diecutter had made the kiss cuts too deep, and SMR's high-speed continuous laser imaging machines jammed about every 1,000 cutoffs, or about 2,000 jams in all. To make matters worse, some labels tore off and got caught in the drum cavity, which slowed production to a crawl and ruined several drums at a cost of about $1,000 each.

Tipped-on cards can be problematic too. If your direct mail job has a plastic or paper card tipped on, don't try to print too close to the edge of the card. Apply the ½-in. (13-mm) rule here as well: allow at least ½ in. between the edge of the card and your intended copy. Less distance is possible, but your mailing services company should be consulted first.

Continuous Laser Imaging Quality Assurance

Companies with high-speed continuous laser imaging printers should have an extensive series of quality control procedures in place. According to Mike Levin, formerly Harte-Hanks Baltimore's operations manager, "Every hour, machines should be stopped, inspected, and cleaned if necessary. We continuously scan for problems such as voids, backgrounding (excessive toner buildup on flash lamps), gray casting, cortron wire toner streaking, bad fusing, poor toner-to-ink registration, and wrong variable image content. In my department, we require every employee working on a job to do hourly signoffs."

Maintenance is another important aspect of quality control. Regardless of whether continuous laser imaging machines are maintained by an in-house staff or a third party, "24/7" coverage (twenty-four hours per day, seven days per week) is essential. Today's direct mail deadlines are so tight that there is little if any scheduling slack. Continuous laser imaging department heads know that if data processing falls behind on a job, every other department will have to scramble to make delivery dates.

Stock and Other Production Issues

If there's anything out of the ordinary with your paper, in general it's a good idea to run a test before beginning the main production run. For example, if you're running either a matte or textured stock through a continuous laser printer, test for proper paper feeding and toner adhesion.

Likewise, if perforations are applied to the stock before laser imaging, make sure they're micro-perfs, or else test. Any glues present must be heat-resistant, or else the end user will end up with a sticky mess. And, just because you use wax-free ink, don't assume that it's laser-friendly. Test all inks first, regardless of marketing claims.

PAL POINT... Laser imaging technology has made terrific advances. It wasn't too long ago that 240 dpi was the industry standard. Now, we're getting to the point where the difference between toner and offset ink isn't all that noticeable. This development has tremendous implications for the future of the direct mail industry.

CHAPTER 29

Inserting Technology

For eighty years, high-volume mail inserting technology didn't change that much. Until recently, "swing-arm" style mail inserters dominated the U.S. lettershop industry and have done so since the early twentieth century. Although swing-arm machines still rule the roost in today's lettershop, a new design is about to ascend the throne. These "continuous-flow" inserters are faster, more flexible, and just as heavy-duty as their predecessors. In short, there's a revolution going on in the lettershop!

Until recently, most high-volume heavy-duty inserting machine manufacturers stuck to their tried and true formula of gathering product and pushing it into envelopes. Although there have been some speed, reliability, and flexibility improvements made over the past half-century, they've been relatively minor. Swing-arm machines have had basically the same design for a very long time.

To be fair, we should mention that a different mail inserter design has been on the market for decades. Unfortunately, for high-volume lettershops, this class of machine is mostly appropriate for office equipment work environments, not industrial manufacturing. Although these lighter-duty machines have some design advantages over swing-arm inserters, they are complex, difficult to maintain, and poorly suited for everyday, high-volume production.

A Revolutionary Design

A recent design breakthrough is reinventing the mail inserting industry. These new continuous-flow machines significantly differ from swing-arm inserters. Consider pocket orientation. When swing-arm machines insert material into #10 envelopes, the inserts travel lengthwise during collation and insertion. On the other hand, continuous-flow machines gather product widthwise, enabling nearly twice as much material to be gathered at the same running speed. And, unlike office-grade equipment, the envelope opening device at the end of the production line is similar to that of the more rugged swing-arm inserter, allowing it to easily keep pace with pocket feeders during high-speed production.

FlowMaster 12000 inserter. *Courtesy Sure-Feed Engineering, Inc.*

These new continuous-flow machines are appropriate for high-volume manufacturing environments for three primary reasons. First, many critical parts are manufactured with industrial grade steel instead of lighter weight materials such as aluminum. Second, like other heavy-duty machines, they are easily adjusted and maintained. Third, the user-friendly, well-designed computer interface uses state-of-the-art electronics.

Under the threat of rising postal costs and an advertising world exploding with competing media alternatives, savvy direct mail marketers understand that they need to offer their clients better returns on their marketing investments. Direct marketers must be flexible and able to go from concept to in-home delivery in what seems like a nanosecond. On the data management side, they need to fully take advantage of data mining and other front-end techniques to maximize response rates. But this is only half of the picture.

Continuous-Flow Technology Benefits

On the production side, direct marketers should look to industry leaders with proven track records on delivering productivity-enhancing solutions made possible by new manufacturing machinery and processes. Speed and flexibility are part of most successful companies' business plans. Continuous-flow inserting machines offer tomorrow's technology today and help ensure that increasingly aggressive in-home mail delivery dates are met. What follows are some specific ways that this is accomplished.

Continuous-flow machines have "downstream shutoff" cascading capabilities. If there's a misfeed, then downstream pockets and the envelope feeder are turned off for that one piece only. By contrast, when misfeeds occur on swing-arm inserters, the whole line needs to be shutdown, corrected, and restarted, which significantly reduces productivity. If a mail component doesn't feed properly on a continuous-flow machine, a "blank" will travel down the line, and the only negative impact will be that the counter will read 10,999 pieces for the hour instead of 11,000.

> **Tech Tip**
>
> Continuous-flow machines cycle 30% to 40% faster than swing-arm inserters and have sophisticated electronic controls that reduce work stoppages by up to 90%. This means that much more mail can be produced in less time with higher yields.

Continuous-flow pocket feeding mechanisms are more forgiving than those typically used in swing-arm units. For example, continuous-flow friction-fed pockets allow you to insert components with just about any fold sequence. Sucker-fed swing-arm inserters can't efficiently feed accordion-folded pieces, but friction-fed pockets offered in continuous-flow units can handle this type of fold with ease. Similarly, Label-Aire attachments pose little threat of creating feeding problems on continuous-flow machines.

When running mailings with generic inserts, continuous-flow machines allow operators to set up "backup" pockets. Then, if the primary feeding pocket runs out of material or jams, the backup will immediately start to feed and will continue to do so until the primary one is reloaded or cleared. This backup pocket feature makes it much easier for operators to get production yields that actually approach maximum cycle speeds all day, every day.

Continuous-flow machines have preprogrammed maintenance reminders scheduled right into the controller. Ignoring mundane tasks like lubrication and the changing of wearable parts is difficult to do because messages flash on the computer screen at regular intervals describing precisely what actions need to be taken. Then the controller automatically records what was done and sets a new alarm for the next scheduled maintenance item. Foolproof maintenance like this translates to less downtime and fewer missed customer delivery dates.

Your Game Plan

Unfortunately, continuous-flow machines aren't cheap. In fact, they're about four times the cost of traditional swing-arm inserters and require better-trained and more expensive operators. Nonetheless, Harte-Hanks Baltimore is planning on future productivity and flexibility gains and increased market demand to at least partially offset higher operational costs. To give you a sense of their collective capacity, Harte-Hanks Baltimore's first six FlowMasters (manufactured by Sure-Feed Engineering, Inc.) can easily yield a million pieces of mail each day. By comparison, it would take about fifteen traditional swing-arm inserters to produce the same amount.

Optional upgrades to a continuous-flow investment are possible. "Intelligent" pockets allow customers to put sort codes on their pieces and selectively insert only the appropriate ones for each recipient by turning pockets on and off without interfering with the all-important mail sort order. For instance, this would allow recipients who have recently bought power tools to receive mail inserts offering drills and tape measures, not pantyhose.

PAL POINT... According to the GAMIS (Graphic Arts Marketing Information Service) report *The Status and Future of Direct Mail*, direct mailers need to "improve the efficiency of the design and creative process and increase its integration with the production requirements of direct mail." On the letter-shop floor, manufacturing flexibility and speed can help direct mailing professionals achieve their marketing objectives. Luckily, the continuous-flow technological revolution is here today.

30 Label-Aire

One of the most frequently forgotten, but extremely versatile, weapons in a direct mailer's arsenal are labels. Label use is virtually endless, limited only by design creativity. The chances are good that the next time you open your mailbox you'll find a label on some promotional piece. If it catches your eye, you'll have technology developed by Label-Aire to thank.

Common Applications

Ever wonder how "live" stamps are applied on direct mail pieces that you know are sent to hundreds of thousands or even millions of people? Label-Aire. What about yes/no stickers; wafer-seals (tabs) closing gatefolded or short-panel folded products; brightly colored labels cheering up black-only text; and foil-stamped, embossed, or debossed labels? Again: Label-Aire.

Have you and your clients found yourselves in this bind: You need color to sell, but your budget only allows for one-color printing? A good compromise might be to apply a brightly colored label on one-color laser-imaged product. You'd get the color you need at a price you can afford.

Maybe your client has twenty-five stores and wants twenty-five different maps leading customers to each location. Since changing your

Tech Tip

Variables affecting Label-Aire production speed and cost include:

- Orientation of the label: (1) landscape or portrait; (2) upside down or right side up
- Proximity of label placement to the edge of the product
- Glue adhesion, especially if label application is over ink, varnish, or other paper coatings
- Multiple-up designs
- Feasibility of inline production yields

plates on press twenty-five times is probably cost prohibitive, perhaps applying twenty-five different labels over a common direct mail piece will allow you to get the multiple lots you need at a price you can afford. Marketers love the versatility that labels offer because many special codes, unique offers, and different attention-grabbing devices can be tested at a remarkably low cost.

Label-Aire is wonderful for correcting your "oops" projects. Here's an example. One of Harte-Hanks Baltimore's clients recently sent in a typical direct mail project. As the data processing work began, the client made a panicked phone call to its Harte-Hanks Baltimore account manager informing him that the sale date was misprinted. Unfortunately, the client had neither the time nor the budget for a four-color reprint and desperately needed leadership. Within hours the account manager had ordered labels with the right dates, and by the time the company was ready to process the job in the lettershop, the new labels were in house and were easily applied inline on folders.

Bottom line: Label-Aire allowed the delivery date to be met without breaking the bank...*and the customer was delighted!*

A Few Technical Tips
Even though today's Label-Aire machinery can apply most labels within $\frac{1}{16}$-in. (1.6-mm) tolerance, every job is different. It's best to involve your mailing services company early in the job planning stage. To prevent mistakes, discuss your job sooner than later and send an accurate representation of the piece prior to ordering labels. Good communication will prevent unwanted production surprises.

Rarely do large mail houses with lots of "redundant" machinery meet up against quantity restrictions. For example, at Harte-Hanks Baltimore, most Label-Aire jobs are run inline with other bindery operations at speeds approaching

10,000 per hour. Large companies routinely accept jobs running into the millions of pieces.

PAL POINT... Whether you need to save a printing job (improper indicia, promotional date, etc.), add a splash of color to an economically printed piece, or get multiple lots, you owe it to yourself to investigate the many benefits of Label-Aire. Like so many other graphic arts processes, it's one of the little things that can put a competitive advantage in the pockets of those in the know.

Inside/Outside Inkjet Imaging on Saddle Stitching Machinery

Where would the direct marketing industry be without high-speed, versatile inkjet imaging? Probably back in the days of paper labels and indiscriminate mass mailings. Improve the effectiveness of your next self-mailer, booklet, or catalog by using today's advanced inside/outside inkjet imaging technology.

Put some muscle behind your one-to-one direct marketing claims. Data mining techniques offer direct marketers vast pools of relevant information about the purchasing habits, preferences, and needs of virtually any target market audience. The first step is to find the right data. The second is to acquire knowledge of inside/outside inkjet imaging technology. The third is to design appropriate personalized communications and promotional materials that make good use of both data and technology.

What's Possible

Let's start with the basics. For years, direct marketers have known that different people respond to different messages. One-size-fits-all shotgun-style marketing methods don't achieve high enough returns to justify high production costs. Inside/outside inkjet imaging allows direct mailers to tailor their communications to address the needs, wants, and desires of their target audiences. Start by including the recipient's name, contact information, and personalized message inside your self-mailing saddle-stitched product.

Pre-filled-out order forms. Design your self-mailers, brochures, and saddle-stitched catalogs with pre-filled-out bounce-back vehicles such as tear-off business reply cards (BRCs) and order forms. Doing so will reduce the amount of response time needed. This is important because saving people as little as a few seconds can make a difference. Response rates will improve if fields such as name, address, and account number are imaged on the BRC or order form. Response center clerks will have less data entry and will be able to process more orders. In addition, illegible handwriting problems should decrease, resulting in a higher percentage of responses that can actually be fulfilled.

Marketing codes. Marketing codes have a wide variety of sales and marketing uses. Customers responding to promotional materials by telephone frequently are asked for a marketing code printed somewhere on the piece. These codes enable easy tracking of marketing effectiveness. Also, prices and special offers can be code-driven and are easily changed as new marketing information becomes available.

Unique offers. Inside/outside inkjet imaging technology allows individual offers to be derived from information contained within individual recipient profiles. Different strings of text can be imaged based on factors such as previous purchasing habits, behaviors, credit history, and geography. For example, if a bank is soliciting new customers, as a purchase incentive it may offer pocket calendars to people with historically low account balances but pocket watches to its most attractive prospects.

Different telephone numbers and website addresses. Offering different service levels to different target audiences is appropriate for some businesses. A good example of this type of customer segmentation occurs in the airline industry. The major airlines have figured out how to enrich customer experiences based on an individual's frequency of travel, degree of loyalty, and profitability. Among other benefits, frequent fliers can use nearly wait-free telephone numbers and may qualify for preferential check-in treatment. Think of your business. If different phone numbers and

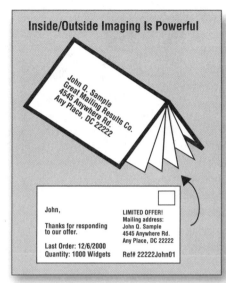

Inside/Outside Imaging Is Powerful

John Q. Sample
Great Mailing Results Co.
4545 Anywhere Rd.
Any Place, DC 22222

John,

Thanks for responding
to our offer.

Last Order: 12/6/2000
Quantity: 1000 Widgets

LIMITED OFFER!
Mailing address:
John Q. Sample
4545 Anywhere Rd.
Any Place, DC 22222

Ref# 22222John01

website addresses would make a difference, consider inkjetting a variable message instead of printing a fixed message. This will reduce production costs and increase your marketing flexibility.

Lower postage. Properly designed inside/outside inkjetting jobs achieve lower postal rates because of longer run lengths. If you consolidate multiple shorter runs into longer ones, your mailings will have more pieces per zip code, qualifying you for better postal rates. For example, consider a million-piece mailing in which your marketing messages are differentiated by inkjetting. Instead of breaking up this job into smaller offset printed batches, keep the entire run contiguous to increase the percentage of your mail that attains the low-cost five-digit USPS rate (150-piece minimum per zip code). Since postage is typically the largest cost component of direct mail, mail as many pieces as you can within the five-digit rate.

Example 1. Assume you're the marketing manager for a financial institution and you want to launch a new "affinity" credit card program targeted at alumni from several universities. The recipients who already hold regular credit cards from you may get gold card upgrade offers. Existing customers without credit cards may get offers to transfer existing credit card balances to new cards. Nonmembers may receive low introductory rate offers. If properly designed, you can vary your marketing message with inside/outside inkjetting, avoiding separate print and mailing runs. This will enable less production time and cost and maximization of postal discounts.

Example 2. A statewide political party could send out personalized saddle-stitched voter guides to likely voters informing them about the records and platforms of candidates in their individual political districts. Again, if a job like this is designed as one run with variable information being achieved through inside/outside inkjetting, production and postal costs will be kept to a minimum.

Tech Tip

When planning your inside/outside inkjet imaging job on a saddle-stitching line, keep all "inside" image areas running parallel to the spine. "Outside" imaging can be oriented in either direction.

Some Technical Tips

Most inkjet imaging production lines have limitations regarding image size, placement, and run direction. Some of these are as follows:

- Inkjet ink is best applied to porous uncoated stock. With extra care and slower run speeds, it's possible to apply inkjet ink on coated paper, but at an increased cost. Solvent-based inkjet ink has inherent problems: toxicity and flammability being among them. Water-based inks are preferred because they're less costly and safer.

- On saddle stitchers, keep variable images on the inside at least 3 in. (76 mm) from the spine.

- Saddle-stitched booklets should have no more than eighteen lines of variable type. Keep these lines in three or fewer groupings of six lines or less. For example, an inside/outside-imaged booklet could contain twelve lines of variable copy on the outside and six lines on the inside, or vice versa. However, having nine lines on the outside and nine lines on the inside is incompatible with most standard imaging equipment. (Contact your mailing services provider for their specific requirements.) In general, there are fewer duplex imaging restrictions on non-saddle-stitched self-mailers.

• Use "closed" signatures because they don't require suction and run faster than "open" ones.

• Make sure your folios are consistent. Most saddle-stitching companies prefer "high" folios.

• Unusual fonts may need to be printed at low resolution. Ask your mailing services provider for advice.

PAL POINT... Lower your production costs and improve your marketing results with cutting edge inside/outside inkjet imaging technology. Combine creativity, a healthy dose of pre-planning, and multifunctional inkjet imaging to yield terrific direct marketing results.

Specialty Direct Mail Products and Finishing

32

Specialty finishing techniques enhance the physical aspects of direct mail projects. Regardless of whether your project looks like a diamond, has a pop-up, or folds in a special way, you've entered the exciting world of specialty direct mail finishing.

When planning a mail piece with specialty finishing, start with a physical representation of the intended product and back into design necessities. Ask your finishing partner, "What are the formats I'm restricted to on the mailer, folder, gluer, and saddle-stitching machine?"

Next, determine how the piece must be printed to suit the needs of the customer. If it is to be laser-imaged, what are the limitations presented because of this requirement? Find a physical form that is capable of meeting your promotional needs yet can be efficiently and automatically produced. The more complex your project, the more you should work backwards from the conceived finished product toward the press and data work.

Finishing equipment and techniques abound in the direct mail industry. One of the biggest potential stumbling blocks is identifying a company that can turn your specialty idea into a physical product. Yes, some specialty machinery is probably necessary, but it's much more important to choose a finishing partner with an artist's eye and an engineer's precision in order to turn your concept into reality.

For example, gluing a shampoo sample onto a piece of paper is no huge feat, but gluing that shampoo sample onto a piece of paper with four-color printing and variable imaging while achieving maximum postal discounts via commingling and drop shipping programs is truly special. Specialty finishing techniques can achieve eye-popping appeal, which may make all the difference when your piece is competing with a dozen other pieces in someone's mailbox.

There are very few cookie-cutter solutions. Instead, this chapter is intended to be a springboard for creativity. If you have a wild idea that you are trying to produce, ask a qualified specialty direct mail production expert for advice. Smart mailing services companies formulate solutions based on available tools and services, even when others say that what you want to accomplish is impossible.

Specialty Products— Explore Your Creativity

Specialty products often take multiple direct mail procedures and combine them with one or more specialty finishing procedures in order to create special physical effects. These types of pieces require careful design and engineering so that they can be efficiently produced and look good at the same time.

> **Tech Tip**
>
> Although an organization may have the basic bindery processes, if it does not have the experience and direct mail skills it may find itself out of its core expertise area. Look for organizations that can provide a history of creating unique products specifically for the direct mail industry and that have all the capabilities under one roof.

Some examples of specialty direct mail products include:

- Saddle stitching with inside/outside inkjet imaging
- Inline selective saddle stitching with inside/outside inkjet imaging
- Laser-printed signatures combined with sample applications in a self-mailer format
- Fully personalized sheets folded and stitched together with generic signatures to create a booklet that combines the cost-effectiveness of lithographic printing with

A Partial List of Specialty Finishing Processes

- Cutting (in combination with another process)
- Folding (in combination with another process)
- Saddle stitching (in combination with another process)
- Trimming (in combination with another process)
- Folding and slitting
- Timed cutting—partial cuts and slits
- Timed perforating—partial perforations
- Glue application—permanent
- Glue application—release/fugitive
- Glue application—remoistenable
- Glue application—pattern
- Pocket creation
- Business reply envelopes (BREs)
- ZIPper perforating
- Label-Aire (in combination with another process)
- Clip sealing
- Sample insertion (magnets, cards, CD-ROMs, and other data storage media, consumer product samples, money)
- Polybagging
- Shrink wrapping

the impact of personalized materials in a colorful package

- Duplex inkjet-imaged self-mailer with integral BRE and reply card
- Self-mailers with items affixed to them for impact or involvement
- CD packaging with uniquely coded inserts, shrink wrapped with an incentive label

If you intend on creating a piece that rises above the ordinary, start with a concept that has some flexibility in size, shape, orientation, etc. Then reverse-engineer the piece starting with the final process and work back. Discuss your project's goals with your finishing partner and ask about their physical requirements. Once they have determined that the piece can be automatically produced, the previous step should be reviewed. At some point, postal regulations need to be assessed. You may find that extensive revisions are required to make the project practical. Finally, you should worry about whether the data will support the required personalization needed. Small conceptual errors can wreak havoc on the bottom line.

PAL POINT... The specialty finishing design process can be streamlined by placing as many processes with as few vendors as possible. In addition, streamlining it also provides a level of confidence that the steps will dovetail correctly, thereby avoiding possible gaps in responsibility and accountability.

Cutting

—with Brenda Slacum, COO, Specialties Bindery

Authors' Note: *For the next four chapters, we're going to delve into the mechanics of four bindery operations: cutting, folding, gluing, and remoistenable gluing. Each is very important to the final appearance of a direct mail piece.*

In direct mail, little things make a big difference. Success depends on good planning and paying attention to small details, like cutting. No matter which portion of the job receives the most attention, every process is vital to smooth production, meeting deadlines, and making money. Think of a beautifully designed but poorly cut piece, perhaps one that has type running "uphill." Anyone who has experienced a problem like this knows what a disaster it can be. Cutting isn't a stepchild; rather, it's vital to success, or lack thereof.

Penny Wise/Pound Foolish

Some graphic arts production companies try to keep as much work in house as possible. Without getting into the pros and cons of outsourcing, do yourself a favor and keep the cutting, bindery, and mailing portions of your jobs together when possible. This will reduce unproductive finger pointing and increase vendor accountability. If a printer, for example, cut a job prior to outsourcing other mailing operations, they have by default accepted at least partial responsibility for the overall quality of the project. If their cutting is off, then so will be the folding, binding, and everything else that happens afterward.

Unlike three-knife trimming in which every side is uniformly cut, flat sheet trimming is difficult to keep precise. What appears to be good cutting during a production run may not be once the product is collated and the binding portion begins. At this point, small cutting variations between lifts may be very noticeable and likely will undermine the high-quality appearance you want. Regardless of whether you're comfortable with outsourcing, at least let those who do your mailing do your cutting too.

Paper and Ink Issues

In general, the harder the substrate, the more difficult it is to cut. Coated sheets with significant clay content have hard surfaces and require frequent knife changes, sometimes as often as twice a day. Recycled sheets can be difficult to cut because they contain a potpourri of paper fibers and miscellaneous waste. When cutting difficult stocks, it's hard to get clean, consistent cuts throughout whole production runs—no matter what precautions are taken. When problems occur, sometimes it's best to make sure your paper is the problem. Do this by substituting a different sheet. If the problem disappears, then it is indeed the paper. Then take appropriate actions.

Some Technical Tips

Draw. The four main causes of "draw" problems are (1) wrong clamp pressure, (2) dull knife, (3) wavy stock, and (4) too thick of a lift of paper. Knives need relief as cuts are made or else sheets will be pulled. Full-sized lifts are fine for most porous stocks, but lift sizes should be reduced when cutting dense, heavily calendered paper with brittle clay fillers. To maintain high-quality standards, lift thickness routinely needs to be reduced by 50%, or even more. Draw problems are

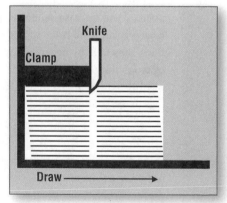

especially noticeable on books with common images bleeding off pages, such as bars or lines. It's very important that printers work with bindery professionals who understand these tradeoffs and are willing to make sure that all jobs are done right.

Trim allowance. Even if your images don't bleed, try to avoid single chop cuts. The inherent problem with chop cuts is that you get one try and that's it. Once the cut has been made, there can be no more adjustments without reducing the final trim size. Cutting problems are magnified and affect folding accuracy and crossover image alignment. Whenever possible, allow at least a ⅛-in. (3-mm) takeout trim margin.

True printers' guide and gripper. As diecutting and foil stamping experts know, easy identification of a press sheet's true guide and gripper saves time and reduces errors. The same holds true for cutting. If a sheet is converted in the same direction as it's printed, registration accuracy is much better. Sometimes guide and gripper sides are obvious, but at other times they're nearly impossible to identify.

Gatefolds. Before beginning a gatefolded direct mail piece, cut a makeready lift, fold it, and make sure the gap in the center is the right size. If the gap is too tight, you can still make adjustments. If it's too large, and there are folds on color breaks, you're stuck. If your cutting services company skips this makeready step, it's like the company is cutting while wearing blinders.

Rotary scoring. When your job needs rotary scoring, score first, then cut. Like die scoring, rotary scoring is more accurate when the true guide and gripper are still on the sheet.

> **PAL POINT...** In recent years, the shortage of highly qualified cutting operators has fueled cutting technology workflow process improvements. Mail shop binderies need to maximize operator productivity to remain competitive. Large companies should consider dual cutting systems for high-volume direct mail work. On some jobs you can eliminate as many as five production people while simultaneously increasing output.

34

Folding

—with Jack Rickard, President, Rickard Bindery

Accurate folding makes a world of difference in the direct mail industry. Look in your mailbox on any given day. Many printing projects with superb ink on paper don't look good because of poor folding. Nothing looks worse than sloppiness—such as folds off color breaks, bend-overs, or wrinkled panels. Coordinate your project with your mailing expert early in the planning stage. Potential folding problems can be prevented—if they are caught early.

Bindery work impacts a direct mail piece's appearance and performance as much as press, prepress, or lettershop work, yet it often is treated as an afterthought.

Plan for Success

Usually there are several ways to run any job. Simple layout changes can produce remarkable time and dollar savings. Panel size alterations and other minor design adjustments can make products look great, function better, and be more compatible with available production machinery.

Many folding jobs should have small variations in panel sizes, but don't. While the shape of individual panels may look similar, often they need to be sized differently to allow for shingling, wraparound, washout (creep), and push-out. Paper is three-dimensional, so don't ignore its thickness. Correctly designed panels will allow your bindery

> **TECH TIP** For roll folds, the outer two panels should be final finished size with each succeeding interior panel decreasing by ³⁄₃₂ in. (2.4 mm). The last panel should be ¹⁄₁₆ in. (1.6 mm) smaller than the preceding one. Failure to perform these steps can lead to bend-overs, bad color breaks, jams, waste and increased spoilage.

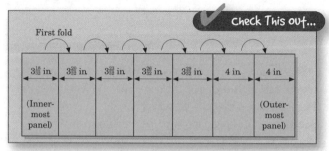

First fold

3⅛ in	3⅜ in	3⅜ in	3⅜ in	3⅜ in	4 in	4 in
(Inner-most panel)						(Outer-most panel)

to fold the product on the color breaks rather than along-side them. What looks like sloppy bindery work really may just be poor design. Physical laws apply to folding. For example, don't expect your direct mail services company to produce an attractive multi-panel barrel-folded piece when equal-sized panels are stripped.

Always provide bluelines, rule-up sheets, bulking dummies, and a marked and sequenced folding sample (first fold A to A; second fold B to B; etc.). Leave ⅛ in. (3 mm) between copy and intended trim position and another ⅛ in. for take-off trim. This allows for natural variation in both the printing and binding processes without risking product damage. Smaller margins are possible, but check first. Allow for washout when folding right angle pieces or when one sheet of paper is slit to nest. Your paper thickness will determine how much washout peeks out. Contrasting colors will make washout more noticeable, but careful preplanning can enhance a product's appearance.

Take Stock of Your Paper

In any product, there is some variation during the manufacturing process. Paper is no exception. Irregularities do occur and will affect folding performance. Inconsistent surfaces will contribute to decreased bindery performance. Even if a paper lot is uniform, there still may be great variation in paper bulk. For example, 80-lb. uncoated cover stock can caliper anywhere from 8 to 13 pt., depending on the manufacturer. This is significant because 10-pt. stock usually folds well, while paper 12 pt. or thicker requires different folding techniques and machines. Be careful of running odd lots. Changing paper in the middle of a job will affect downstream folding, so be sure to mark the change spot and advise your postpress partner.

Generally, the thicker your stock, the more variables you will face. Pre-score your stock if it is 110-lb. text weight or heavier. Sometimes thicker stocks without critical color breaks can be in-line wet-scored or folder-scored, but always ask for an opinion before bypassing diecut scoring.

When folding stock thicker than 10 points, watch for ripple cracking on buckle folders. A knife folder generally will not ripple crack unless the stock is extremely thick, causing the sheet to fracture as it bends around the rollers.

Also, know your grain direction. Reduce cracking and the need for pre-scoring or inline wet scoring by folding your first fold with the grain. If this isn't possible, consider choosing a stock with short fibers and "off machine" coating for better moisture control.

Paper fibers can break during folding and result in cracking. Often, choosing proper fold-plates, machines, and production techniques can save jobs. The shock load on paper fibers increases geometrically with machine speed. So, when

General guidelines for scoring.

Offline channel scoring is recommended if your:

- Stock is 110-lb. text, 65-lb. cover, or heavier.
- Job's height/width or width/height ratio is greater than 3:1. (When thin rectangular sheets travel down a folding machine's side guide, they become unstable as they're jogged to the thin side. This is true regardless of the number of scores on a piece.)

Examples of width/height and height/width ratios

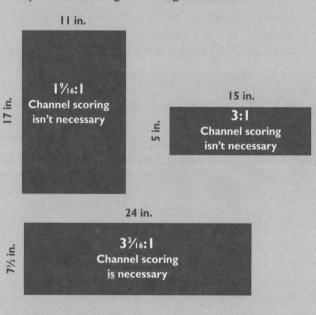

Channel scoring isn't necessary if your:

- Job is printed on 90-lb. text or lighter, folds with the grain and has a height/width and width/height ratio of 3:1 or less.

Get scoring advice if your stock is:

- 100-lb. text or 60-lb. cover.
- 90-lb. text and folds against the grain.

fibers are breaking, slowing down your folder greatly reduces fiber stress and many times eliminates the problem.

Ink Can Sink Your Job

If ink is too brittle, it may crack. Correcting this problem is difficult because ink has neither the strength nor flexibility of paper. Choose your fold plates and folding machines to minimize paper stress, add moisture to the surface (wet score), and slow down your folder. Wet ink is another common problem. If there is a good chance of having wet ink at bindery conversion time, use varnish or aqueous coating. Protecting jobs with reflex blue, metallics, or heavy black ink coverage resting against white paper after folding usually reduces smudging, scratching, and marking.

Varnish: Hero or Villain?

First, the good news: Varnish seals ink and prevents marking and smudging.

Now, the bad news: A varnished sheet's surface is slippery and fold rollers have difficulty getting a good grip. Varnish dries to an uneven surface of peaks and valleys. When sheets run through folder rollers, the peaks are knocked off and ground into powder that gets on the rollers and alters their gripping ability. The exact point at which the rollers get a solid grip on the buckling sheet determines the position of a fold. If there is any change in the gripping characteristics of the rollers, the fold moves.

When a folding operator begins running a job, the rollers are clean and the job runs well. However, after a few thousand pieces, varnish powder is deposited on the rollers and begins to change the fold position. A knowledgeable operator will stop, clean the rollers, and watch the fold return to its proper position for another few thousand sheets. Or, a different operator may stop, change the fold stop position in the plate, and watch the piece quickly go out of folding register again. Either way, productivity and quality are very difficult to achieve on long-run jobs with full (flood) varnish. For example, a non-varnished job that runs at 10,000 pieces per hour might yield only 6,000 or 7,000 if varnished.

Folding Potpourri

• Both wide- and small-gap gatefolds are possible. If you need a gap smaller than ⅟₁₆ in. (1.6 mm), or larger than a few inches, ask.

• "Green" projects can cause production problems. Soy ink tends to scuff more than regular petroleum-based ink. Recycled paper has a tendency to have less strength than pre-consumer paper because of shorter paper fibers, and it affects bindery perform-ance. Recy-cled paper tends to be less pliable and is sub-ject to more jams, increased tearing, a poorer quality fold, and more wrinkles.

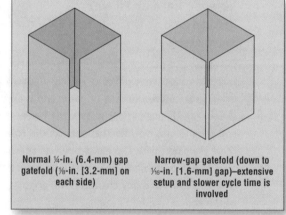

Normal ¼-in. (6.4-mm) gap gatefold (⅛-in. [3.2-mm] on each side)

Narrow-gap gatefold (down to ⅟₁₆-in. [1.6-mm] gap)–extensive setup and slower cycle time is involved

• When using slitters, always check for clean edges. Asking your bindery about edge sharpness on multiple-up or folder trimming jobs is appropriate. For good product appearance, do not use rotary knives to trim final folded enamel stock thicker than 0.024 in. (0.61 mm), or offset thicker than 0.028 in. (0.71 mm).

• For presses with dryers, consistent drying time is important because either oven temperature or web speed variation will lead to paper pliability and brittleness fluctuation.

• Allow your folding services company also to cut your job. You will substantially decrease transit problems and increase your yield.

• Properly band your skids to avoid shipping problems. If the stretch wrap is too tight, product corners can be damaged. For coated stock, band at right angles.

PAL POINT... Differentiate your direct mail projects with good folding. Be sold on the fold. Your customers are.

35

Gluing

—with Jack Rickard, President, Rickard Bindery

Many direct mail projects involve the application of glue, even if it is trimmed off during final conversion. Gluing is another behind-the-scenes bindery process that truly impacts direct mail production. Successful gluing requires a scientific approach and an artistic touch. The four horsemen of gluing—paper, ink, coatings, and glue—are about equal contributors to a job's success. Their combinations are nearly infinite, and unexpected results do frequently occur. Sometimes easy-release (e-z) glue tears paper fiber. Sometimes permanent glues perform like easy release. Even the wizard Merlin would be puzzled.

Graphic arts glues are mainly oil-, resin-, or latex-based. Each type performs as expected most of the time, but there are more exceptions than anyone would like. Since glue is so important in many direct mail applications, we're going to explore production issues that can hinder project success.

Both easy-release and permanent oil-based glues offer good adhesive properties and are appropriate for physically heavy or varnished pieces. However, their relative great bulk may result in unattractive product from a marketing viewpoint. Resin-based permanent glues are cold-applied and provide a good bond with a relatively small amount of residue. Latex easy-release glues are thin, generally reliable, inexpensive to apply, energy-efficient (applied cold), environmentally friendly, and FDA approved for many food packaging applications. However, latex is a natural rubber tree product and coagulates when contacted by steel, iron, or plastic. Coagulation can cause machine applicator problems. Also, latex glue doesn't work well in compressed air applicator systems.

Easy-Release Glue (a.k.a. Removable or Fugitive)

Easy-release glue performs well 19 out of 20 times. But one tough job will prove there's no easy release from gluing headaches.

Easy-release glue performs best on penetration-resistant, highly calendered, dense paper with heavily inked and coated

Common uses for easy-release glue.

- Easy-release glue is an economical and attractive substitute for wafer sealing. (Properly manufactured products work great in the U.S. mail.)

- It keeps foldouts and gatefolds from unravelling during binding operations.

- It holds products together so that they can be automatically inserted (i.e., consumer product instruction sheets into bottles or boxes).

- It is great for pharmaceutical and/or miniature folded products.

surfaces. Matte and other lightly calendered enamel stock, offset paper, or sheets with a heavy clay fill are susceptible to delamination and fiber tearing when the intention is an easy-release effect.

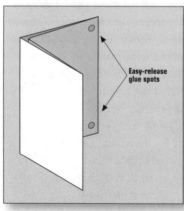

Easy-release glue spots

An example of easy-release glue being used with a three-gatefold (also known as a "double gate") product.

Latex easy-release glues require long setup times (three to four minutes) and tend to spread when the opposing sheet is tightly squeezed. Their curing period is really twenty-four hours, even though they appear to be dry after ten minutes. Unfortunately, products that perform properly ten minutes after manufacturing can change in twenty-four hours and pull fiber. Oil-based easy-release glues have a shorter curing time, but glue bulk remains an issue.

Managing variable adhesion and chemical reactions is important. Some easy-release glue solvents, such as ammonia, dissolve aqueous and other coatings and result in unintentional permanent adhesion. Occasionally, permanent resin glues can function as easy release on aqueous coatings because when dry they become very brittle and perform better than latex or oil-based easy-release glue.

Permanent Glue

Permanent gluing problems do occur, but they are infrequent. For best results, select a paper with a porous surface and position the glue away from ink and coatings. Permanent glue needs to bite into paper, so the harder the surface, the more difficult it is to penetrate the sheet and create good adhesion. Knock out ink, varnish, UV, and aqueous coatings wherever you place permanent glue because glue tends to rest on top of coatings and cannot penetrate and grip fiber.

Permanent resin glue spreads on stocks and coatings with a high barrier to penetration and can result in a poor bond or sloppy glue coverage. Absorbent and porous paper will allow glue to penetrate paper fibers and produce a strong bond. If gluing must occur over ink coverage, use wax-free ink. When stuck with a difficult permanent gluing job with aqueous coating, as a last resort try

Tech Tip Often jobs require custom-made glues for special situations. You may need glue to penetrate a tough aqueous coating, work in high humidity, hold in freezing and thawing situations, or bind folded plastic while in a washing machine. A responsive supplier can save you hours of fruitless experimentation and help you meet deadlines.

using ammonia-based latex easy-release glue instead of permanent. It might just work.

Since water-based resin glues spread, those with

critical glue registration require constant monitoring and sample pulls during production. Take special care when applying resin glue in a trim-out area. If glue reaches the paper's edge, sheets will stick together. Conversely, if glue spreads too far into the piece, it will not be removed during the final trimming process. If a trim-out area is shorter than ⅜ in. (10 mm), consider using easy-release instead of permanent glue because negative consequences of excess glue spread are less.

Machinery/Supplier Issues

Prior to the 1970s, gluing wasn't widely viable. Electronic systems that sense the presence of a sheet, wait a specified period of time, and then apply glue have made gluing practical. Most systems on the market now have pretty good electronics, but the next big advance in gluing technology is almost here.

Today's air-activated, noncontact permanent gluing systems are extremely accurate and remarkably trouble-free. The capability to apply permanent glue from the bottom of a sheet is useful.

If your mail services company does gluing, make sure it is in frequent contact with its glue suppliers. Since most glue has a short shelf life, purchase and use glue biweekly to ensure good adhesive properties.

PAL POINT... Increase your likelihood of success. If you aren't gluing on a daily basis, get expert advice before beginning critical jobs.

Remoistenable Gluing

—with Jack Rickard, President, Rickard Bindery

Until the 1990s, sheetfed printers had little opportunity to sell products with remoistenable glue. Today, short-run direct mail jobs with remoistenable glue are practical because the current crop of machines yield great quality and good production. Both sheetfed and nonheatset web printers now can produce products with direct response reply devices and participate in profitable direct mail campaigns.

There are primarily two ways of applying remoistenable glue. The older technology—cold application of water-soluble remoistenable glue—works by transferring glue to paper by either a wheel or a blanket. This process has two main advantages. First, heat by itself doesn't activate it, which means it is downstream laser compatible. Second, glue application "pads" can be different sizes and run in different directions, which allows the efficient manufacturing of products such as three-sided "U" bar reply devices and stamps.

Unfortunately, there are some significant drawbacks with cold-applied glue. First, it has to be run through hot dryers, which frequently cause excessive paper curling and cracking. Second, cold adhesives tend to be thicker right at the beginning of the glue strip. Sometimes this thick buildup takes longer to dry and forces operators to choose between having either brittle paper or semi-wet remoistenable glue that may stick to neighboring sheets. Third, a potential fire hazard is created when conveyors stop running, if there is any paper in the oven.

Extruded Glue

Hot-melt extrusion is the other way to apply remoistenable glue. These types of machines give operators more control over the placement and appearance of glue strips as they're

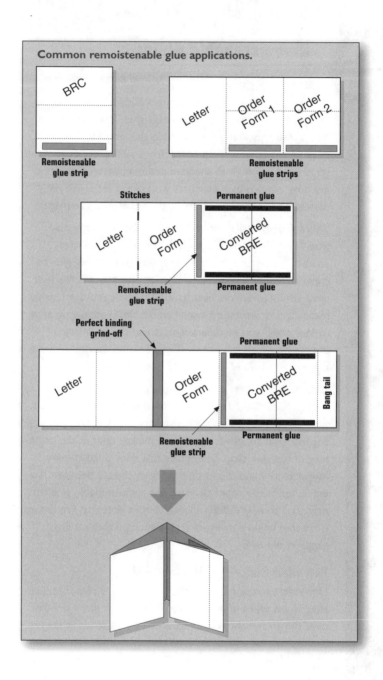

Common remoistenable glue applications.

being applied to the paper. Computer-controlled solenoids allow operators to precisely start and stop glue flow wherever necessary. For example, if a two-up piece is being glued on an 8½-in. (216-mm) side, an extrusion machine will detect the presence of paper and begin the glue flow ½ in. (13 mm) away from the paper edge. Then it will apply glue for 8 in. (203 mm), stop for ½ in., apply glue for another 8 in., and finally stop the flow ½ in. away from the trailing edge.

Water-soluble glue applied on a pattern gluer can do this too, but since pattern gluers rely on timed entry rather than motion sensors, its application isn't as precise. In addition, extrusion hot-melt glues rarely curl paper and generally have a professional appearance while cold-applied glue looks duller, may have ragged edges, and tends to curl since moisture is being added to only one side of the sheet.

A potential drawback of extrusion machines is that they can only apply remoistenable glue in parallel lines. This means that glue laid down in the shape of a "U" either needs two passes or two machines running inline at right angles to each other.

Inline Application

Many remoistenable glue jobs are done inline with other binding processes. For example, they may apply remoistenable glue, stop-perforate the sheet, apply seam glue to form a pocket, fold it (barrel folds, accordions, and gatefolds), apply wafer seals, slit it, and keep the job in

> **Tech Tip** If you have a form with side-by-side envelopes, don't have the glue strips rest against each other as they're coming off machines. Unintentional adhesion can occur when glue strips are directly in contact with each other face to face, especially during shipping. Staggering designs so that glue strips avoid contact with each other is a much better way to plan a job.

mail-sort order—all inline. Needless to say, inline production greatly reduces turnaround times and cost, making non-heatset web and sheetfed companies competitive on many jobs. Regardless if the piece is a self-mailer or will be bound into another product, inline production is a good value.

Avoid flatbed trimming after remoistenable glue application because it may cause a series of three problems. First, productivity will decline because sheets will have to be cut in very small lifts in order to clamp properly and not tear due to inadequate clamp pressure. Second, glue bulk will raise a bump in each lift, resulting in the top sheets being longer than the bottom ones after trimming. Third, cutting through remoistenable glue wreaks havoc on knives, especially those super-hardened for long life.

PAL PoINT... Remoistenable glue makes many direct mail programs better. Printed pieces with easy ways to respond are more effective than those without. In summary, remoistenable glue makes response mechanisms easy and quick to use.

37

Matching, Bursting, and Converting High-Volume Mailings

Here's a question that doesn't need a rocket scientist to answer: If the goals of a marketing program can be accomplished at either low or high cost, which is better? (Hint: We're looking for a three-letter word here.) To be successful at keeping your costs low, do yourself a favor and involve a direct mail planning expert early in the conceptual stage, especially when working on new matched mailing projects.

Savvy marketers are always on the lookout for ways to tweak their project specifications to get the most bang for their direct mail buck. In many instances, personalization and message customization help increase response rates. However, if matched mailings are poorly designed, production costs can spin out of control. In today's competitive direct mail landscape, there isn't much wiggle room for layout mistakes—so get it right!

Let's assume you're working on a routine million-piece four-page 8½×11-in. (216×279-mm) solicitation letter with personalization on each page. Your layout can make a big difference in terms of production costs. The best way to attain high-speed/low-cost production on this type of job is to position pages one and three side-by-side on a 17×11-in. (432×279-mm) form. This allows your mailing services company to image the pages, take the roll to a document converter, slit and cut the sheets to final size, and marry and fold it all in one pass, thereby giving you a completely folded four-page form. On the other hand, if pages one and four are laid out side by side, then the forms must be slit apart and page four turned before continuing the marrying and folding operations. Although still relatively common, this mistake incurs extra setup time and slows down machine production rates.

Now let's turn our attention to a matched mailing project with six personalized pages. Depending on the capabilities of your mailing services provider, your best option likely will be to print all sheets sequentially and stream them together offline. If printed, coded, and sequenced properly, you won't need to use expensive scanning equipment to verify proper component match. Coding is especially desirable when some pages are personalized with fields that are difficult to verify during production. Examples of hard-to-verify fields are last purchase, previous donation, and current promotional offer. Conversely, examples of easily verifiable fields are standard ones like name, address, or customer number. Large mailers routinely mail eight-page personalized letters with conventional equipment, but for projects with more pages, additional planning is usually required.

Form Separation

Separating forms used to be a standalone and relatively costly process. However, machinery advances in folding and other inline processes have significantly contributed to making form separation faster, less costly, and more efficient. Regardless of whether your forms are imprinted roll to roll or fan-folded, they need to be separated. In most cases, fan-folded forms are "burst" apart, and roll-to-roll forms are cut apart on document converters.

Since continuous roll-to-roll technology has established a competitive foothold in high-volume mailing production, the need for bursting apart fan-folded forms at their perforations has been reduced. Most marketers would like to avoid bursting in the first place because this process leaves noticeable perforation marks unless extremely fine micro-perfs are used. In general, pin-fed bursting is fast and cost-effective as long as folding and conversion processes occur inline.

Bursting equipment doesn't allow you to take out head and foot trim margin inline, but fortunately, document converters don't have this limitation. Document converters, such as those manufactured by Bowë and others, are much more flexible than bursters, which explains their widespread industry dominance. Unlike bursters that burst apart forms, document converters use knives to cut forms apart. If you can spare the paper and slight reduction in manufacturing speed, two-knife production with take-out trim offers slightly better quality than single-knife chop cuts.

There are still some applications where bursting equipment outperforms document converters. For example, consider a project that needs a personalized $8\frac{1}{2} \times 3\frac{1}{2}$-in. ($216 \times 89$-mm) form to be matched with an $8\frac{1}{2} \times 11$-in. (216×279-mm) letter. If a "slit-to-nest" format isn't possible (i.e., different stock, printing issues, etc.), then the forms need to be imaged during separate runs. An efficient way to produce this type of job would be to run the $3\frac{1}{2}$-in. piece eight-up on a 17×14-in. (432×356-mm) form with a stack sort data layout, burst them apart, and flatbed trim final-sized pieces while keeping proper mail sort order. *(Note: The stack sort layout allows cutting operators to keep final-sized product in matched order by just cutting the bursted forms in predefined stacks.)*

Now, if your 11-in. (279-mm) letter and $3\frac{1}{2}$-in. (89-mm) matched mailing insert were on the same stock and could be printed on the same form, the best way to run this job would be to place both on an $8\frac{1}{2} \times 14$-in. (216×356-mm) sheet, gatefold, and slit the piece (slit-to-nest). This completely eliminates the matching of separately printed components. Yes, "intelligent" inserters with barcode readers can accomplish this same result, but why spend the additional money? In general, high-volume matched mailings are most efficient when personalized components are printed on common forms and converted inline while keeping proper sort order.

Cutting Edge Technology

For mailing jobs with multiple matched components, intelligent inserters or sophisticated inline conversion machines deserve consideration. As an example of how powerful the later can be, it's now possible to simultaneously image, trim, fold, tuck, glue, marry, and insert up to seven personalized components. While there are different ways of accomplishing this feat, it's only practical for very large and frequently repeating matched mailing jobs.

There is another class of equipment specifically designed to handle statements with randomly varying page counts. These "statement converters" are appropriate for credit card statements, phone bills, or other similar types of mailings. With the help of end-page record locators, sophisticated scanning technology, and holding "reservoirs," statement converters can easily handle a one-page credit card bill followed by a seven-pager and then a three-pager. These machines are investment-intensive and usually involve cut sheets, not continuous forms.

PAL POINT... The three most important words in direct mail are "test," "test," and "test." Developing and implementing a continual testing strategy is critical to the success of high-volume mailing campaigns. Personalization, manufacturing costs, and mailing class choices are all significant factors. Just as you need to test the effectiveness of five-digit versus carrier route rates, consider testing different levels of personalization. Some companies have discovered that avoiding unattractive carrier route markings is the best way to increase profits. Some people have learned that deeper levels of mail customization do the same.

Polybagging

—with Mark Beard, President, Finishbinders

Nothing gets printed pieces through the mail more safely, attractively, and inexpensively than polybagging. Companion pieces can be bundled together—big or small, thin or thick —in virtually any order, while maintaining proper mail order sequence.

Polybagging is just at the beginning of its growth curve in the U.S.; in Europe, it's already everywhere. There, promotional materials, newsletters, magazines, and many other printed materials have been polybagged for years.

The polybagging process isn't complicated. The polybag is formed over stacked product and heat-sealed on the front, back, and top as it travels down a conveyor belt.

Polybagging Design and Production Tips

• Before printing your address panel, remember that indicia and address label positioning usually runs *parallel* to the spine edge of normal-sized mailings—not adjacent.

• More and more polybagged packages now contain personalized content. These projects must be carefully planned.

• While it's not mandatory, try to have your carrier (bottom) piece be the largest and sturdiest of the package.

• The polybag seam is usually between 1–2 in. (25–50 mm) wide. For aesthetic purposes, it can be positioned to suit your needs, but there are limitations, especially when printed poly is involved.

• Chop seals on both ends of your polybag need an allowance of at least ½ in. (13 mm) each for excess film. This requirement increases proportionately as the bundle gets thicker.

• Before applying paper labels directly to the polybag, insist that your polybagging services company test adhesive strength prior to production. Poly film is a petroleum-based product and can have complicated glue adhesion properties.

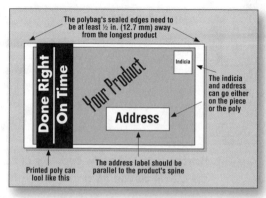

The polybag's sealed edges need to be at least ½ in. (12.7 mm) away from the longest product

Done Right On Time

Your Product

Indicia

Address

The indicia and address can go either on the piece or the poly

Printed poly can lool like this

The address label should be parallel to the product's spine

• For printed poly, keep metallic inks away from sealed edges.

• If your mailing project is unusual in any way, play it safe by getting a pre-production sample approved by your local postmaster.

Costs

For all but the smallest runs, polybagging is inexpensive. If makereadies are spread over 100 pieces, polybagging costs a lot. So does everything else. At about 2,000 pieces, polybagging starts to make sense. Once you're doing 10,000 or more, other protection methods seem impractical. For example, inserting materials into large paper envelopes costs a lot more and, many would agree, doesn't look as nice. Even the fastest automated shrink wrappers rarely exceed 2,000 pieces per hour, while polybagging machines can routinely run at 20,000 per hour, depending upon insert number and size.

Common direct mail applications for polybagging include the following: promotional materials, newspaper inserts with free samples, magazines packaged with accompanying pieces, computer publications with free software, piggybacked periodicals, atlases with maps, subscription renewal notices, brochures, statements, and invoices.

Polybagging Benefits

Polybagging has a lot going for it:

• **Versatility.** Since a polybag is built over stacked product, you have much more flexibility when midstream job changes happen. For example, if a thick insert needs to be added to a portion of a polybag project, pre-purchased envelopes may not be usable. However, with polybagging, your project should be fine. Also, since polybag shuttle feeders and loading pockets accommodate wide varieties of object shapes and sizes, many consumer products may automatically be fed. Similarly, conveyers can turn pieces at a right angle. Therefore, spine and folding edges no longer need to run parallel with the polybag seam.

• **Clear packaging.** Polybags let the beauty of printed pieces show through packaging. Paper envelopes cost more and hide the package's contents. Sometimes this is a good thing, but often it isn't.

• **Advertising.** Printed poly film looks great.

• **Automation compatibility.** The USPS approves some poly films for full postal discounts. No longer do you need to sacrifice mailing savings for polybagging benefits.

• **Protection.** While the most common polybag films are 1 mil and 2 mil, 4-mil film or thicker can be used. Excessive moisture and banging around wreaks havoc on traditional packaging. Some companies have enclosed polybags into fertilizer bags. Try that with paper envelopes!

TECH TIP

Polybag ink registration is terrific. Today's register marking systems, machine clutches, and servomotors guarantee that your message appears at the same place on each bag.

- **Environment.** 100% recyclable poly is now widely available.

- **Downstream automation.** At the end of the polybagging line, automatic sorting, stacking, and strapping makes for easy entry into the mail stream.

- **User friendliness.** Easy-to-open perforated seams are commonplace.

- **Technology.** Spot glue that keeps pieces in place, blow-ins, selective pockets, and inkjet imaging are all widely available.

- **Thick bundles.** Your total polybag thickness can be well over 2 in. (51 mm).

Printing on Poly

The economics of printing on poly film are like those of printing on paper. Either way, short-run, four-color jobs are expensive, but printing costs decrease as run lengths increase. Halftones, PMS colors, metallics—you name it—all look great on poly. If security is an issue, opaque inks with knocked out mailing areas ensure that polybagging is as safe as opaque envelopes. Proxy statements, financial information, and other projects that require security are well served by polybagging.

PAL POINT... If you're still skeptical about polybagging, verify its power for yourself. Go to your local post office and watch people interact with their mail. Notice a lot of unopened envelopes getting tossed? Sure. What about polybagged packages? They get opened—nearly every time.

39

Mail Security*

Direct mailing professionals know that their number one job is to get recipients to open the envelope sent to them. With fears of bioterrorist agents, your jobs have become more difficult. No longer is the color of the envelope or design of the insert the only element of a mailing that you must consider. Now, vigilance to safety and security throughout the business world has helped to shape a new paradigm for direct mailing professionals.

Communicating credibility is a top priority. Methods to ensure the safety and security of direct mail documents can be used at each stage of the process—from printing to production to the actual mailing. One of the most telling indicators of credibility is the method by which the mailing is posted. Metered mail and permit mail allow the recipient to ascertain the identity of the sender with or without opening the letter or package.

However, only digitally metered mail includes special security features. The metered barcode acts as a digital fingerprint, with data regarding the sender embedded in the code. The system has inherent credibility because the information-rich indicia imprint is traceable to the meter owner. With software technology available today, the contents of each mail piece are highly controlled, highly secure against errors and tampering, and highly verifiable. A combination of technologies makes it possible to track every piece of letter mail from origin to destination. Even mailings that qualify for bulk rates can be metered—as opposed to printed—with postage.

---

*Adapted from Pitney Bowes "Securing Your Mail System," reproduced with permission, Pitney Bowes, copyright 2002.

Direct mailers need to take an active role in the management of their mail centers and those of their vendors.
The mail center is the informational hub of every company, and individuals working in it have direct impact on both incoming and outgoing mail. In fact, mail center staff serve multiple roles—from gatekeepers to information resources. In order to ensure that these employees are capable of dealing with all aspects of mail security, each should be thoroughly screened. Mail center employees have access to sensitive information, including details about the financial and personnel status of other employees. By using legally approved screening methods, such as drug screens, criminal background checks, and reference and employment history inquiries, you can be assured that the mail center staff is equipped to handle its responsibilities. Since many of their tasks require specialized knowledge, all mail center employees should be continuously trained; updating procedures and informing staff of new developments to ensure all mailings comply with federal regulations. For example, Pitney Bowes employees continually receive training to better secure the mail environment, including the identification of potentially hazardous letters and packages and protocols for handling suspicious mail. Having the right people for the job and applying the right procedures can significantly minimize mail security risks.

Outsourcing is one way to manage the direct mailing process. Because of the commitment that mail center management requires, some companies decide to outsource this function to professional firms that specialize in on-site training and technical support. Working with these consultants, you can improve accuracy and efficiency through trained staff and the latest mail production technologies. In addition to staffing and equipment, consultants can help perform an audit to ensure that your mail center is properly access-controlled and that only authorized personnel handle the mail. Going one-step further, direct mailing professionals can also choose to outsource all mail center functions. The company's outsourcing can be done on or off-site, depending upon your needs.

Other things to consider. In addition to the use of metered mail, a secure mail center, and outsourcing experts, direct mailing professionals should always consider the reaction of the recipient when designing their mailings. Status-quo processes may need to be changed if they can in any way be perceived as a security breach. For example, the use of antisetoff powder (cornstarch-based slip agents and talcum powders) during the printing process triggered enormous concern as recipients of magazines and catalogs assumed the fine powder was a contaminant. In this case, direct mailing professionals may need to eliminate the use of antisetoff powder or find a viable alternative in order to assuage the fear of recipients. Here is the takeaway message:

> *All direct mailings must instantly communicate that the sender is credible and legitimate—from the inclusion of a company logo, return address, or alternative contact information (e.g., toll-free number, website address) to a cellophane window that allows recipients to view the contents of the envelope.*

All of these elements contribute to a new class of "intelligent mail" that is tailored to meet the needs of senders and recipients. The key is for direct mailing professionals to design and forward mail in a safe and secure manner that encourages the recipient to open the materials. With the partners, technology, and resources available today, it is very easy for you to get the assistance you need to do so.

PAL POINT... Use a postcard to inform your customers and prospective customers about the steps you've taken to secure your mail center and the mail they receive from you.

4

Direct Mail
Post-Production

SECTION

CHAPTER 40

Commingling

Are you trying to squeeze out more direct mail cost savings? Is there a faster way to get your mail to its destination? If someone said there is, would you be interested? If you think this is the brainchild of a snake oil salesman, it's time to learn about today's new "commingling" technology.

For the right types of jobs, commingling paired with drop shipping significantly reduces postal costs, gets mail into homes and businesses faster, and provides better test marketing results. As of now, only a handful of North American mailing companies offer commingling services.

Companies that segment very large mailings into different cells should consider commingling technology. The financial services and non-profit sectors frequently can reduce overall production costs and shorten delivery times while increasing market-testing accuracy. During the era of large "shotgun" mailings, postal discounts were easy to achieve. Today's highly targeted "rifle" mailings have increased response rates but have also reduced the percentage of mail that qualifies for five-digit postal discounts.

Perhaps you have a credit card client offering sports-oriented cards. If only one

> **Tech Tip** Commingling is the process of merging multiple zip strings into a single mail stream. When the right types of jobs are combined, significant postal discounts can be attained. The United States Postal Service (USPS) requires 150 pieces per zip code as the minimum quantity to achieve desirable five-digit postal discount rates. Commingling shorter runs together improves the chances that more zip codes reach this 150-piece threshold. Although "synergy" is an overused buzzword, it accurately describes the commingling process.

"all-sports" credit card is promoted, there may be enough targeted prospects in most zip codes to qualify for the five-digit rate. However, if recipients are segmented into sports enthusiast categories such as tennis, softball, bowling, skiing, and golf, postal costs will increase as more mail is pushed into the higher three-digit rate. Luckily, commingling allows you to keep segmentation benefits while maintaining lower postal rates.

Assume you have a for-profit mailing segmented into three cells. If zip code 99999 has 150 pieces—50 in each lot—all mail in this zip code will be charged at the three-digit rate. However, if the three lots are commingled into the same tray, then all 150 pieces qualify for the lower five-digit rate, saving $1.95 in postage ($2.25 if nonprofit) at 2001 postal rates. If you have a million-piece for-profit mailing of which 75% benefits from commingling, then the net savings passed on to you after all commingling costs could be more than $5,000.

Evaluation and Production

If properly done, commingling will remain transparent to the client. The first step of any project should be running a pre-sort on the data file to predict savings, because some jobs simply won't realize any benefit. For example, if you have a million-piece mailing and 95% of it already qualifies for the USPS five-digit rate, the cost of commingling outweighs the savings.

Once in production, presorting projects is important. If your million-piece mailing's pre-sort determines that 20% of the job qualifies for the five-digit rate without commingling, this portion should be processed first so that commingling costs aren't applied to 200,000 pieces. Next, the remaining 800,000 should be data-processed and staged in the warehouse by lot and zip code order. Then, job A should be loaded onto the commingling machine in zip code sequence followed by jobs B, C, etc.

Even though high-speed commingling machinery accommodates hundreds of zip codes at one time, most commingled jobs still need to be split into multiple runs. Prior to running a commingling job, statistics of each lot need to be downloaded into the commingling machine's computer. If there's a mismatch between expected and actual mail for any reason (i.e., spoilage in the letter shop), commingling systems will track this information.

Test Marketing

Since multiple cells of a job arrive at destination SCFs in the same trays at the same time, test-marketing results are more accurate. For example, if four different color envelopes and three messages are being tested, mail from all twelve cells going to zip code 99999 will be simultaneously processed. A traditional multiple-cell mailing not only costs more, it's more susceptible to skewed testing results because of variable delivery dates.

Other Considerations

Before deciding in favor of commingling your next job, consider a few factors. Commingling requires additional coordination time, especially if one company's job is piggybacked onto another's mail. Even though commingling services companies process huge volumes of mail each month, they still need about three to five extra production days for most commingling jobs. Multiple-cell mailings on a specific day are possible as long as different cells of the same job are married together. Mailings that need to be commingled with other jobs usually are given a three- to five-day drop range.

Once the commingling process has begun, it's virtually impossible to stop. First, commingling jobs are data-processed differently, and second, mailing rates for all jobs are interdependent on each other. Since stopping a job from entering the mail stream can only be done by hand, it is highly impractical—without even considering the lost postal savings anticipated for the other lots. If there's any realistic chance that a mailing will be halted, commingling isn't for you.

Also, if a commingling job needs to piggyback onto another, there has to be work in the pipeline. To use an analogy, it's hard to hitchhike when the road is empty.

PAL POINT... O For the right high-volume mailing professional, combined commingling and drop shipping cost savings can be eye-popping. Saving tens and even hundreds of thousands of dollars is just a good start. For some direct mailers, commingling is definitely a "have-your-cake-and-eat-it-too" proposition.

Drop Shipping

Do you need your mail to arrive faster, more predictably, and at a lower cost? Would you like to eliminate as many USPS processing stages as possible? An efficient and cost-effective drop ship program may be the solution. Since the cost of drop shipping frequently is less than the accompanying postal savings, it's like your direct mailer pays you to handle your mail!

If this sounds too good to be true, rest assured that many large-volume mailers are achieving great results right now.

What Is Drop Shipping?

The USPS offers significant discounts in exchange for delivering mail directly to "destination" postal facilities. Long ago, the USPS decided to embrace the concept of work sharing, which means that postal customers can achieve discounts for reducing USPS processing time. Companies that presort, use automation-compatible imaging (barcoding), and transport mail as close to the final destination as possible (i.e., drop ship) will achieve the largest postal discounts.

Most direct mailing companies prepare the mail as best as they can and deliver it to a local (origin) USPS facility. Mailing companies that take advantage of drop ship discounts will bypass their origin post office, section center facility (SCF), and bulk mail center (BMC) by delivering mail directly to destination SCFs and BMCs throughout the country, thereby saving a bundle in postage costs.

To maximize postal savings, direct mailing companies need to run full tractor-trailer loads of mail, and this often requires combining drop-shipped mail from several mail runs. Mailing companies without a critical mass of direct mail volume are forced to either run LTL (less than truck-load) trailers or have them leave too infrequently—neither of which is good for customers. If too many LTL trailers are used, freight costs will exceed postal discounts, and the only winners will be trucking companies.

There's More to Drop Shipping Than Cost Savings

Less USPS handling means mail gets to its destination faster and more predictably. Bypassing the local post office, local SCF, local BMC, and destination BMCs means that there is a lot less chance for mail to be delayed. On average, drop shipping will save between three and seventy-two hours per bypassed USPS postal facility. If four facilities are bypassed, up to eleven days of processing time variance will be eliminated.

Drop shipping allows direct mailers to segment certain portions of the country, which means they have better control of "in-home" dates. For example, if you want a homogeneous drop date for your mailing, drop shipping allows you to schedule all mail so it arrives at destination SCFs and BMCs throughout the country at or near the same time. Although no one can control when destination USPS facilities actually process the mail, less postal handling means that the range of home delivery dates will be narrowed. On the other hand, if you are concerned about overloading your response center capacity, you may want to stagger your in-home dates. Drop shipping allows control of when mail is delivered to destination postal facilities so an avalanche of simultaneous responses doesn't flood response centers.

In addition, drop shipping offers better test marketing control, and tracking ability. Since truck manifests clearly show mail routes, determining when a piece of mail is delivered to destination postal facilities is easy and accurate. Drop shipping allows mail to become "modular," so all trays and pallets are fully traceable—each piece of mail belongs to a tray; each tray belongs to a pallet; each pallet belongs to a truck. This level of tracing isn't possible without drop shipping.

Outsourcing Drop Shipping Services

When outsourcing drop ship services, ask your direct mailer to perform a data file analysis to determine how much your job will benefit. Some projects just aren't a good fit for drop shipping and an up-front analysis can prevent a lot of wasted effort.

Your mailing services provider should process your data to achieve maximum drop shipping and postal savings. Large companies that send out regularly scheduled trucks throughout the country can "overlay" the transportation schedules of work already in house over the data of a proposed job and accurately calculate drop ship savings. Once production on a job has begun, staging it in a drop ship order that matches jobs already in house will maximize postal discounts for all involved customers. For example, if your mailing has only 10,000 pieces going to Boston, piggybacking it onto another truck with the same destination may prevent LTL shipments for several companies.

Mailing Companies "Pay" You to Process Your Mail

Often, mailing processing costs are far less than the accompanying postal savings. This means direct mail companies essentially "pay" their customers to process mail. Take a look at the following two actual examples of Harte-Hanks

Savings Examples

Harte-Hanks Baltimore Nonprofit Customer	Client 1	Client 2
Pieces mailed	6,000,000	6,000,000
Pieces drop-shipped to destination SCFs	4,000,000	325,000
Savings/1,000 pieces @ 2001 postal rates	$24	$24
Savings per each mailing	$96,000	$7,800
Pieces drop-shipped to destination BMCs	2,000,000	175,000
Savings/1,000 pieces @ 2001 postal rates	$19	$19
Savings per each mailing	$38,000	$3,325
Total postal savings	$134,000	$11,125
HH-Balt mailing and shipping costs	$47,000	$3,069
Total net savings to customer	$87,000	$8,056
Net savings per 1,000 pieces	$14.50	$16.11

Baltimore customers. Client 1 is a nonprofit customer that runs four large mailing jobs each year and nets annual postal savings of nearly than $350,000 on these jobs alone.

Client 2 is another nonprofit that mails smaller regional jobs and typically saves at least $7,500 every month that they mail. Client 2 saved more per 1,000 pieces because its mail is sent only to a limited geographic area (East Coast). These are real examples of organizations that greatly benefit from drop shipping. In short, drop ship savings can be a tremendous competitive advantage if properly planned and executed.

PAL POINT... Drop shipping programs are not for everyone. Some companies insist that their mail must enter the USPS postal stream on a particular day, regardless of impact on in-home delivery dates. Those who need the security of a postal receipt showing that mail was delivered to a postal facility on a particular day shouldn't use drop ship services. However, for the fastest delivery, most production control, and maximum postal savings, drop a few hints to your direct mailing partner about drop shipping your next large mailing job.

Materials Handling/Logistics

The best direct mail professionals are on a never-ending quest for the fastest, cheapest, and sexiest solutions.

Companies that convert product from one form to another need good materials handling and warehouse management processes. In addition to performing data processing, commingling, and drop shipping services, direct mailers take physical job components and add value by cutting, folding, addressing, stitching, and otherwise changing the shape and form of mailing components. However, getting good machine production is only part of the operational equation. If machines are operating at peak efficiency (fast production, low spoilage, good quality, etc.), but are held up because of poor material flow, the end result is bad productivity rates.

Due to the complexity of many direct mail projects, attention to detail is very important. Small companies that employ fewer than 100 people may be able to get along without computerized inventory tracking. Past this size, these systems often are essential. Without state-of-the-art materials handling systems, large companies can, and often do, waste countless hours looking for missing components, pallets, etc.

Materials Handling Tips

• **Strapping and wrapping.** All pallets should be properly strapped and wrapped. Coated stock with a slippery surface can, and sometimes does, slide off pallets. When this happens, re-stacking the job is a costly and time-consuming affair. Don't cut corners: Strap and wrap all pallets well.

• **Double stacking.** Pallets with paper should not be double-stacked. No matter how careful forklift drivers are, damage will occur. Compensating for bent or crushed

corners increases the amount
of time required to load
machines and reduces
productivity.

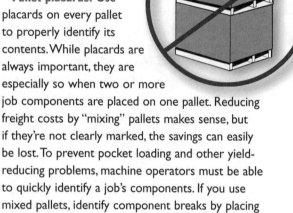

• **Pallet placards.** Use
placards on every pallet
to properly identify its
contents. While placards are
always important, they are
especially so when two or more
job components are placed on one pallet. Reducing
freight costs by "mixing" pallets makes sense, but
if they're not clearly marked, the savings can easily
be lost. To prevent pocket loading and other yield-
reducing problems, machine operators must be able
to quickly identify a job's components. If you use
mixed pallets, identify component breaks by placing
separators between the material—especially when
the components look the same.

• **Carton packing.** Choose the right carton size and
gauge and pack all boxes tightly. "Transit" marking—
spots where ink is scuffed or partly rubbed off—is
the result of excessive product movement during
shipping. For example, if a 12-in. (305-mm) tall box
is filled 11 in. (279 mm) high, product will jostle and
rub as trucks turn and go over bumps. Even if poorly
packed jobs escape transit marking problems, they
still may end up with bent corners, thus causing
machine jam-ups, reduced yields, and increased
manufacturing costs.

• **Ink issues.** Be careful of direct mail components
with heavy ink coverage on one side of the sheet and
light coverage on the other. Any time a lot of ink

rests against white paper, the chance of undesirable marking increases, either during shipment or pocket feeding. The problem is even worse when reflex blue is used because it dries so slowly. Other inks causing concern include some reds, purples, and metallics.

• **Print less.** If direct mail project managers and their business partners pay careful attention to materials handling issues, spoilage will be reduced. After a few months of consistent and documented spoilage reduction, it may be possible to reduce print quantities by a percentage point or two.

Advanced Racking Technology

Racking is a type of materials handling and warehousing system with many benefits. Although companies pay for the cubed volume of their buildings, frequently they don't use all their available floor-to-ceiling space. Advanced racking technology allows forward-thinking companies to house materials all the way up to the ceiling without stacking pallets or damaging product. Going up, instead of out, reduces forklift travel distance, thereby saving time and labor hours. Racks bolted into cement floors also serve to protect pallets from errant forklift damage.

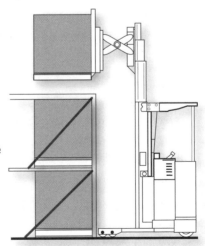

Harte-Hanks Baltimore's warehousing needs increased a lot in the late 1990s. Its 50,000-sq.ft. (4,650-m^2) warehouse once could accommodate only 3,000 pallets. However, a $300,000

investment in a state-of-the-art racking system increased the capacity to 7,500 pallets in the same space. Although this investment sounds expensive, it was a whole lot less than putting up a 75,000-sq.ft. (6,970 m²) addition to the warehouse.

Racking systems with special "narrow aisle" forklifts reduce aisle space needs, thus allowing more racks to fit in less space. Some only require 10-ft. (2.5-m) aisles between double rows of racks instead of the customary 12 ft. (3 m).

If any of your vendors are thinking of installing a new racking system, encourage them to buy one that uses a standard 40×48-in. (1.02×1.22 m) pallet size. Doing so means you won't have to worry about coordinating any production changes between your vendors.

Mailing Choices Matter

Commingling and drop shipping mail reduces floor space requirements and consequently saves direct mail customers money. If jobs are commingled together, companies can reduce their pallet needs as much as 70%.

For example, assume you have three jobs, each using 100 pallets with postal trays stacked four high. Without commingling, 300 pallets will be needed. If the three jobs are commingled together, the average postal tray height might increase to twelve per pallet, reducing the number of required pallets to 100. Eliminating 200 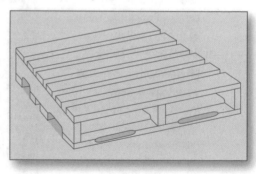 pallets is significant because much less labor, floor space, wrapping materials, paperwork, and consumables (such as forklift fuel) are needed. According to Brian Smith, Harte-Hanks Baltimore's warehouse and facilities manager, "commingling and drop shipping together cut warehousing costs in half."

PAL POINT... Many businesses treat their warehouse like an unwanted stepchild. Although materials handling is ripe with potential costs savings, frequently it's last on the resource priority list. This is a mistake, because good product flow is vital for efficient manufacturing. In short, effective materials handling processes lower direct mail costs.

PLANET Codes

Direct mailing professionals need timely deliveries and good information. To help, the USPS has developed a "PLANET code" system that allows mailers to track how their projects are doing as mail processing occurs. Then, real-time decisions can be made to improve both current and future results.

The PLANET code concept began when the Postmaster General created the Mailers Technical Advisory Committee (MTAC). This organization's mission is to develop solutions that mutually benefit postal customers and the USPS. MTAC developed PLANET codes, and although the system has been operational for first-class and standard letter mail for a while now, it just went online for flats in the summer of 2001.

What Are PLANET Codes?

A PLANET code is an additional barcode usually placed within the address area that identifies the job, mailing services company, and postal client. As PLANET-coded materials pass through automated postal equipment, transactional data is captured, stored, and returned to the mailing services company. For instance, if PLANET-coded mail enters the postal stream at the Washington bulk mail center (BMC) and flows through a California BMC, section center facility (SCF), and destination delivery unit (DDU), processing data will be captured at each of these four postal facilities.

Let's consider two types of PLANET codes—"destination confirm" and "origin confirm."

If postal customers want to track their outbound mail, they need to use destination confirm codes. This allows them to know the status of their mailing at any particular moment and make reasonable assumptions about in-home delivery by zip code. For example, if mail has just been scanned at a destination SCF, final delivery most likely is two to three days away in most geographic areas. Or, if it just traveled through machine casing equipment at a DDU (local post office), a reasonable assumption is that delivery will occur within three to eight working hours. When using destination confirm codes, typically they need to be applied on only a few pieces of mail per zip code.

On the other hand, if you need to track the response to your mailing as it's happening, use origin confirm codes on every mail reply device. For example, when a mail recipient in Sioux Falls, South Dakota, responds by dropping a coded BRC (business reply card) in the mail, you will know exactly when the local post office begins return processing. This gives you a heads up as to how strong your response will be. If early indications are that you're getting a good response, you can make operational decisions such as ramping up response center staffing or ordering more product to meet anticipated demand. If initial response to a limited-time promotion is lower than expected, perhaps you can boost your campaign with more promotional activity. Either way, with the use of origin PLANET codes, you can reasonably expect about a two- to three-day advance warning about what's happening.

According to Charley Howard, a founding member of MTAC and a Harte-Hanks vice president, origin PLANET codes can also be used to pay bills. It works this way: When a consumer receives a bill with an origin PLANET code on a reply device and mails it, as soon as it is processed on the first automatic postal processing machine, relevant account information is immediately "pushed" to the billing company and the payment is recorded. Since the physical piece of mail is now obsolete, it is pulled from the mail stream and thrown out, simultaneously streamlining the bill payment process and reducing postal traffic.

PLANET Codes in Use: Three Examples

Example 1. A major U.S. retailer frequently mails marketing promotions in quantities ranging between 20 million and 30 million pieces each. Since these mailings are very time sensitive, the retailer needs to know that its mail arrives at destination in the right timeframe. Since this company is a long-time MTAC member and has been using destination PLANET codes since their inception, the retailer has built up a wealth of postal data pertinent to its needs. It has discovered patterns of mail processing problems and have taken two concrete steps to improve mailing performance. First, the company changed its mail preparation and drop shipping sequences to compensate for problematic delivery areas. Second, they've given the USPS tremendous amounts of mail flow data so internal problems in the system can be fixed.

Example 2. A national wholesaler was experiencing low response rates on promotional mailings to resellers and needed to take corrective action. Since its mailings were only about a million pieces each—relatively sparse for nationwide delivery—and were delivered primarily to rural areas, management thought was that slow USPS delivery might be to blame. However, when destination PLANET codes were applied and results compiled, the wholesaler discovered that the USPS was

From the USPS site www.planetcodes.com:

Like POSTNET code, planet code has 12 digits and consists of tall and short bars. PLANET symbology is the inverse of POSTNET:

Each POSTNET digit hs two tall and three short bars.

Each PLANET digit has three tall and two short bars.

All PLANET barcodes include a five-bar checksum digit (or correction character). This digit is always the number which, when added to the sum of the other digits in the barcode, results in a total that is a multiple of 10.

PLANET also supports alpha encoding. Two-digit-numeric combinations represent the entire alphabet:

Alpha	2-Digit Number
A–I	11–19
J–R	21–29
S–Z	31–38

POSTNET		PLANET
‖ıⅼıı	0	ıⅼ‖‖
ıⅼ‖‖	1	‖ⅼıı
ıⅼıⅼı	2	‖ıⅼı
ıⅼⅼ‖	3	‖ıⅼı
ıⅼıⅼı	4	‖ıⅼı
ıⅼⅼı	5	‖ıⅼı
‖ⅼıı	6	‖ıⅼ‖
‖ıⅼı	7	ıⅼ‖‖
‖ıⅼı	8	ıⅼ‖ⅼı
‖ıⅼıı	9	ıⅼⅼ‖

doing a pretty good job of getting mail to destination on time. Armed with this new information, this company began changing its mailing creative and promotional offers. It quickly saw better results.

Example 3. One of the big three U.S. credit bureaus got involved with PLANET codes for a different reason. When people request copies of their credit reports, by law they have to receive them within a specified time period. Prior to using PLANET codes on outbound credit reports, this bureau generated and mailed a second one whenever customers complained about non-receipt. Now the bureau accesses PLANET code data while the customer is on the phone and explains exactly where the report is within in the mail system. In addition to significantly decreasing the amount of duplicate reports generated, they stop most complaints dead in their tracks.

Select a mailing services partner that knows how to apply codes, process mail to meet your specific needs, capture PLANET code data from the USPS, convert it into meaningful reports, and give you feedback in a timely manner. Regardless of whether you need staggered in-home dates or simultaneous mailings, choose a company that can help you in either case. You need a mailing services partner with a wealth of knowledge about the U.S. postal system and the ability to adjust its mail preparation sequences, commingling, and drop shipping schedules to suit your needs.

PAL POINT... Demand better information. The USPS isn't always proactive in revealing its problems, but at least it has developed the PLANET code system to help mailing professionals develop work-around solutions. Start taking advantage of USPS PLANET codes and expect better results.

CHAPTER 44

Response Management

Before your mailing has been sent, and certainly before any responses have been received, it's critically important to have a carefully constructed response processing system in place. This is the mechanism that ensures that the prospect receives timely communication while the request is still relevant. Regardless of what type of fulfillment is required—more product information, telephone call, sales visit, etc.—timeliness of response is where some direct response programs go awry.

For many years the response process has been heavily tilted toward business reply cards and envelopes. Now, telephone calls to toll-free lines and Internet responses generate significant amounts of traffic.

When planning a response management system, a reasonable first step is to compile a response database. Ranges of options are appropriate for differing circumstances such as:

> **TECH TIP**
>
> It's important to choose unique number strings carefully. They must be unique, not too long (creating the possibility of more input errors) and should not be a direct representation of anything the recipient might perceive as being confidential—i.e., telephone number, social security number, date of birth, etc.

• **Capturing responses from scratch.** This unsophisticated system requires data entry personnel to enter the full name, address and other pertinent information on the reply device. In almost every case, this is a poor use of your database and is subject to lots of data entry errors.

• **Unique identification number.** Using a unique identification number saves both money and data entry time while vastly improving information accuracy. Unique identifying numbers—sometimes referred to as "finder numbers"—should be placed somewhere on each record and on the BRC, if there is one. Upon receipt of the response, only this number is required for entry and the appropriate record automatically is called up.

• **Barcodes.** If your goal is to remove all initial keying activity upon receipt of the response, print a barcode on the BRC. To fulfill the request, scanners automatically will read the unique identification number and retrieve the record.

• **OCR readers.** With the advent of affordable processing power and sophisticated OCR (optical character recognition) software, fully automated response systems are becoming commonplace for some applications. If properly executed, these OCR-based systems allow the response forms to be automatically scanned, completely eliminating manual data entry. Then, fulfillment activities can begin with as little human intervention as possible.

Response Analysis

As requests are fulfilled, all captured responses should be tabulated and analyzed. This is the point at which direct response advertising differs from traditional advertising. Here, the direct marketer begins to review the specific results of the specific mailing and overall campaign. Tabulating overall response rates and calculating "cost per response" figures are necessary to determine effectiveness and profitability.

After analyzing many campaigns, direct marketers can create mathematical models that anticipate response, cost per response, and financial return, all things being equal. This principle is at the core of the direct marketing field, regardless of marketing vehicle used. Payback is easy to determine.

Regardless of whether you're analyzing a single mailing or a multiple-year campaign, tally all costs associated with the outbound mailing including list acquisition, creative, production, and postal costs. Next, calculate gross inflow of revenues. Then, subtract all response costs including variable labor, cost of goods sold, fulfillment, and allocation to overhead. Lastly, do the math.

An appealing aspect of direct mail is that cost per response can be positively identified, unlike many competing mass-market advertising vehicles. Based on what the numbers say, determine your next step. If subsequent mailings are appropriate, the numbers will tell you. Regardless of whether you're satisfied with your return, start testing your mail components versus your previous best pulling piece.

PAL POINT... Test everything. Allow no sacred cows. Test the envelope, creative, headlines, fonts, inserts, shapes, printing, colors, everything. Each time take the response and compare it to the best performing piece in your arsenal. Perhaps one of the best things about the direct mail and direct response industry is that the numbers don't lie. Over time, you will become armed with the vital information you need to drive exceptional marketing performance in the future. Good luck, wherever you are in your quest for direct response excellence.

APPENDICES

Appendix 1

General Questions for a Typical Direct Mail Campaign

1. Mailing quantity _____

2. Frequency _____

3. Mail class _____

4. Envelope: ❏ Yes ❏ No (if no, skip to #13)

5. What size is the envelope? ❏ #10, Business
   ❏ 5⅞×9 in. ❏ 9×12 in. ❏ Other: _____

6. Is envelope a window? ❏ Yes ❏ No

7. How many inserts?

   #1: _____

   #2: _____

   #3: _____

   #4: _____

   #5: _____

   #6: _____

   Which insert is addressed? _____

8. Product size _____

9. How is it addressed? ❏ Cheshire label ❏ Inkjet
   ❏ Laser ❏ Other: _____

10. Is there an indicia? ❏ Yes ❏ No (metering required)

11. If laser-imaged, is there a sample or mock-up including
    stock type? ❏ Yes ❏ No

12. Is data manipulation required? ❑ Yes ❑ No

13. How many files? ❑ Tapes _____ ❑ Diskettes_____
    ❑ CD-ROM _____ ❑ Other: _____

14. Are there different mail pieces (splits)? ❑ Yes ❑ No

15. Address accuracy: ❑ No ❑ Yes—no adjustments
    ❑ Yes—with adjustments

16. Is there just a name and address, or is there a client
    code, VIN #, etc.?

    _____

    _____

17. Are there any required special reports?

    _____

    _____

Notes:

• If a mailing is metered, postage money should be
  required before production begins, since meters
  need to be replenished.

• If approvals are required, please note in the job
  specifications.

• Nonstandard data reports can be generated. There
  are fees for each, and they take time to perform.
  Advance notification is important.

• Uppercase/lowercase conversion is possible, although
  it is not 100% accurate. For example, some names
  like "MacArthur" may result in "Macarthur."

• Even small data projects require an ample amount of
  time to set up; therefore expect minimum charges.

Appendix 2

Sample Job Checklist

Client/Job _____   Job No. _____

❏ Sales notified

❏ Quote sent

❏ Mail date established

❏ Schedule completed

❏ Tape disposition

❏ Material disposition

❏ Job confirmation sent

❏ Signed job confirmation received

❏ Tapes/files received

❏ Postal permit

❏ Drop-ship required

❏ BMC/SCF report received

❏ Drop-ship spreadsheet created

Data Processing

❏ Convert sheet submitted

❏ Group I sheet submitted

❏ NCOA acknowledgment sent

❏ Merge/purge sheet sent

❏ Order for match mailing checked

❏ I have reviewed the convert

- ❏ I have reviewed the presort
- ❏ I have checked the presort report for proper containerization/palletization
- ❏ Postage request sent
- ❏ Samples have been printed/run

Laser
- ❏ I have a signed proof letter
- ❏ Quality checkpoint sheet submitted to Data Processing

Material
- ❏ All delivery receipts double-checked
- ❏ Quantity received sufficient for job + spoilage
- ❏ Inventory spreadsheet created

Mail Plant
- ❏ Postage received
- ❏ Sample board and/or set-up samples submitted
- ❏ I have approved, signed-off samples
- ❏ I have/am receiving production QC samples
- ❏ Daily production spreadsheet created
- ❏ Samples have been sent
- ❏ Spreadsheets are being updated daily
- ❏ Spoilage is being kept and scanned daily

Job complete: Date _____
Job billed: Date _____

Appendix 3

Sample List of Required Information

All accounts must have the following information assembled into a file or notebook.

Basic Account Information

- Internal contacts (names, phone numbers, fax numbers, addresses, home phone numbers)
- External contacts (names, phone numbers, fax numbers, addresses, home phone numbers)
- Store/market/versions
- Numbers
- Addresses—hard copy and PC- or mainframe-compatible media
- Overview of client purpose/history
- Overview of job process
- Pricing
- Billing

Details of Job Processing

- Typical job steps, program names, flow charts, expected input tapes
- Area for potential problems
- Verification/quality control checkpoints
- Previous problems and solution

Reports/Output

- Report names, program names, when to run, samples
- Report distribution
- Verification of reports

Documentation

- Copies of tables—hard copy and PC or mainframe compatible
- Sample run sheets from job set-up
- Sample special forms or requests
- Sample mailing pieces

Appendix 4

Sample Quality Checkpoints Form

Use this form in conjunction with the live laser sign-off approval submitted to your Data Processing department for laser imaging. This form should note specific characteristics of the form and copy like the following: "If XX copy is used in the Johnson box, body copy in paragraph two should read XX" or "if address is in Texas, then home logo must appear at bottom right of form," etc.

Once this form is completed, attach a live laser sign-off.

Quality Checkpoints

Client/job _____

Job no. _____

Date submitted _____ / _____ / _____

(Use yellow marker on live laser to highlight checkpoints and circled numbers to identify location of checkpoints.)

Form _____

Font_____

Copy _____

Unique elements_____

Color _____

Size/shape _____

List/geography _____

Must get right _____

Required sign-offs _____

Appendix 5

Incoming File Preparation

Develop internal policies that you need in order to effectively process incoming files. This means listing all media that you can accept, and keeping it current. Also, make sure your storage procedures are written so that no customer data is ever lost or misplaced.

Sample Data Policies

1. All incoming customer tapes, disks, cartridges, etc., will be kept in our tape library and unless clients specifically request the return of their media, they will be deleted after 90 days. It is extremely important to make the customer aware of this policy. Be sure it is on every quote and confirmation.

2. A record layout and estimated quantity must accompany each and every file we receive, including email files. Remember the record layout is our road map to what is on the file or tape. Without it we don't have enough information to proceed. Our clients do not need to guess about record layout.

Sample List of Acceptable Media

Account managers for direct mail services companies should know exactly what file formats and media types are acceptable to their data processing department. A sample list may look like the following:

- IBM 3480 cartridges, compressed or uncompressed
- IBM 3490E cartridges
- Mag tapes (reel/round tapes)—1,600 or 6,250 EBCDIC or ASCII
- IBM/PC-compatible data

- ZIP disks
- Diskettes—write protect all diskettes; use Excel to test for readability
- CD-ROM
- Electronic transmission—email, Internet, FTP

Converting Files

Many computer systems have certain programs that are used over and over again. Your mailer may repeatedly use presort, list hygiene, and merge/purge programs. These programs are set up to look for specific data—such as last name or street address—in a specific place on every tape. If a tape has not been converted to a "standard format," that data may not be in that specific place and the program may not produce accurate output. Therefore, data processing departments need to convert each tape to a common format so their programs know where to look for each specific piece of data.

Record Layout

A record layout is essentially a "map" of what is on a file or tape. It shows the location of data within each record, which must be in the same place in each record. It shows the length of each field and the type of data (alpha or numeric). Every file or tape received must be accompanied by a complete and accurate record layout. Files shouldn't be converted without one, and good mail shops have a "no exceptions" allowed policy.

There is no more important part of any job than converting the file. If this is done incorrectly, the entire job will be wrong. What's worse, it may not be immediately apparent that an error was made. It is important to be very careful when giving data processing conversion instructions.

Information must be exact. All other stages of a job will be based upon what has been converted and where it was placed afterward.

What to Convert

It is essential that direct mail account managers understand what their customers are trying to accomplish in order to properly instruct the data processing department on what to convert. They need to be clear about what data will be used and how it will be used. Don't forget about how this data might be used for result tabulation. Will there be codes to capture? Should there be an account number? How about a match code or barcode? Again, be fully aware of how the data will be used in order to convert a file properly.

Personalization

If you need to create laser-imaged letters, be sure to get clear instructions on how the salutation and address area should look. Should the salutation be Dear Mary Jones, Dear Ms. Jones, or Dear Mary? Is there a salutation field in the file? Will your data processing department need to isolate the first and last names to make salutation? Is there a title field? Should the job be run through the gender-assign program?

Sort Order Is Important!

If a job is to be run multiple-up, the data must be processed in an appropriate order. "East/west" imaging (first name left, next name right, etc.) will cause problems because the stacks will be out of order after final trimming. Instead, "north/south" ordering allows jobs to be processed, separated, and married with the job ending up in proper mailing sequence.

However, if a job is to be commingled, then the data needs to be sorted in straight zip code sequence. For mail that is to be drop-shipped, but not commingled, processing needs to be done first by zip code order and second by destination SCF (section center facility) and BMC (bulk mail center).

Bundle breaking is applicable when other auxiliary functions such as match mailings will be performed.

Appendix 6

De-Dupe Merge/Purge Form

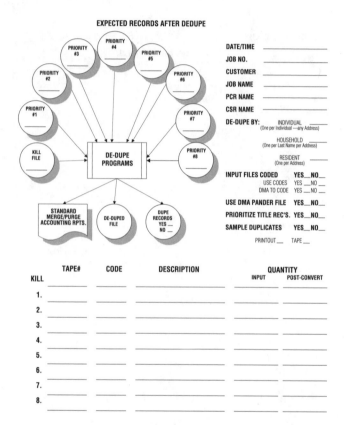

EXPECTED RECORDS AFTER DEDUPE

PRIORITY #3
PRIORITY #4
PRIORITY #5
PRIORITY #2
PRIORITY #6
PRIORITY #1
PRIORITY #7
KILL FILE
DE-DUPE PROGRAMS
PRIORITY #8

STANDARD MERGE/PURGE ACCOUNTING RPTS.
DE-DUPED FILE
DUPE RECORDS YES ___ NO ___

DATE/TIME _____

JOB NO. _____

CUSTOMER _____

JOB NAME _____

PCR NAME _____

CSR NAME _____

DE-DUPE BY: INDIVIDUAL _____
(One per Individual —any Address)

     HOUSEHOLD _____
(One per Last Name per Address)

     RESIDENT _____
(One per Address)

INPUT FILES CODED   YES__NO__
   USE CODES   YES __NO __
   DMA TO CODE YES __NO __

USE DMA PANDER FILE YES__NO__

PRIORITIZE TITLE REC'S. YES__NO__

SAMPLE DUPLICATES   YES__NO__

   PRINTOUT __   TAPE __

	TAPE#	CODE	DESCRIPTION	QUANTITY	
KILL				INPUT	POST-CONVERT
1.	_____	_____	_____	_____	_____
2.	_____	_____	_____	_____	_____
3.	_____	_____	_____	_____	_____
4.	_____	_____	_____	_____	_____
5.	_____	_____	_____	_____	_____
6.	_____	_____	_____	_____	_____
7.	_____	_____	_____	_____	_____
8.	_____	_____	_____	_____	_____

Courtesy Direct Marketing Associates, Inc.

Appendix 7

Merge/Purge and Data Manipulation Questions and Answers

Merge/purge is so important to reducing postal costs that it deserves additional mention. Here are some commonly asked questions and answers about this vital data processing service.

Q: What is a merge/purge?

A: Merge/purge is the technique used to combine names, addresses, and related data from various mailing lists to identify and potentially eliminate duplicate names for a single mailing or to create a marketing database.

Q: Are all merge/purges pretty much alike?

A: Actually, they're not. The merge/purge from one service bureau (or in house computer service department) to another has differences.

A good merge/purge will:

- Save money.
- Provide you with control over the definition of what constitutes a "duplicate."
- Eliminate "real" duplicates yet not eliminate names you want to mail to (causing an "overkill" situation).
- Identify multiple buyers within an organization.
- Handle "eliminate," "suppress," and "fraud" files.
- Improve the printed appearance of the names and addresses.
- Give all the reports and statistics that direct marketers need for dealing effectively with list brokers and managers and making good future decisions to increase mail effectiveness.

- Prioritize lists.
- Be completed correctly and on time.

A superior merge/purge will also:

- Process all North American data instead of being country-specific.
- Increase response rates.
- Be both parameter-driven and flexible enough to meet all data needs.
- Carry all the information throughout the merge for future use.
- Provide reports showing examples of records that were dropped from the merge/purge.
- Allow customers to change data parameters after the merge/purge has been completed.

Q: Isn't there more to merge/purge? Specifically, what else should be looked for? What are the subtle differences?
A: Look for a data services company whose merge/purge programs can perform these "miracles" during processing:

- Use different criteria for determining duplication between business and consumer records.
- Correctly de-dupe records such as "IBM," "International Business Machines," and "Int'l/Bus Mach," for example.
- Use multiple techniques of matching during processing. For processing efficiency, some records are "exact matches" and others require more sophisticated algorithms.
- Search for duplicates with phonetic equivalency, similar spellings, common data entry errors, and transpositions. It should also have the capability to search within a postal code, a region, a state/province, or country for duplicates.
- Assign a male or female code to a record based on first names, exempting certain names like "Pat" or "Robin."

- Generate a city and state from a zip code.
- Link business firms throughout the nation.

A: The best way is to ask your direct mailing services partner for a printout of at least 5,000 records from your data file in a four-up Cheshire format, with name, title, company, division, address, city, state/province, and zip code/postal code printed on the labels. Examine it. Look for duplicates. Get a general idea of what's on your data file and then ask for recommendations as to how to handle particular challenges such as:

- What is the best technique for determining duplicates for this file?
- How should address components be separated and identified?
- What techniques should be used to identify businesses, professions, institutions, etc.?
- How should marginal (possible) duplicates be identified? Then, what procedures should be implemented to make the best decisions?

A: The techniques used in North America (U.S. and Canada) to identify duplicates and possible duplicates include these:

- Mathematical equivalency
- Phonetic matching
- Multiple duplicate search
- Address patterning
- Unique business file patterning

- Linkage of firms throughout the nation
- Flexible matching criteria
- Identification of "possible" duplicates

Q: I've heard of a "match code" system. What is it used for?

A: Match codes, which are still used by many systems, were used by the first merge/purge systems as a standardized, simplified method of purging "exact" duplicates. This system takes a portion of each major field (such as the first three consonants of a last name, the first three letters of a street name and street number, and your postal code) and assigns this as your match code.

This method is adequate in many applications. However, the art and science of duplicate and possible duplicate identification has developed so that it includes other techniques of finding the duplication possibilities within a file or between multiple files.

Match code systems are still adequate to de-dupe many exact matches where the name and all address components are exactly alike. However, if there's not an exact match, name and address processing programs can have features that search for "maybe" matches. This is accomplished by determining how closely the various components of name and address records have to match for them to be considered duplicates.

Q: What is a "maybe" match?

A: Assume two records are electronically compared and found to be 98% alike. Are they duplicates? Probably. What if they are only 75% alike? Are they still duplicates? Maybe yes, maybe no. Provide maybe match instructions to your mailing services company. If you aren't sure what it should be in your case, ask for advice.

Q: What are two primary variable matching techniques?
A: Variable matching techniques come in two main categories. The first is the "point scoring" method in which elements are assigned numerical values. A second is the "dial" method whereby parameters or values are set in the program. This second approach compares similarities and differences in key parts of the record and determines the percentage or degree of match between one or more names and address records.

Both of these methods determine duplicate records based on their "conclusions." In addition to checking records in the same zip code or town, they can be set to compare records in BMC districts, states, or provinces.

Q: How important is it for a computer service bureau or in-house data processing department to edit the data provided to them from another computer house for a merge/purge?
A: Don't assume that the data provided to you has had the proper merge/purge processes done to meet your data requirements. Most companies involved with the capture, manipulation, and transference of data have different needs and use formats suitable to their own purposes.

The merge/purge software that your service bureau or in-house data processing department uses should provide extensive editing capabilities to determine the accuracy of the provided data prior to the merge/purge. This crucial step adds discipline to the file and ultimately determines the final success of the merge/purge process. Some of the editing of data that should be done include:

- Street name standardization and spelling correction
- City name spelling correction
- Postal code validation, assignment, and correction
- Title code and job title standardization
- Identification of company names

When choosing a service bureau or software vendor for your in-house data processing department, determine the degree and type of data editing that should be performed before each file is submitted for the final merge/purge or to a database assembling process.

Q: What are the different techniques used by a computer service bureau to determine which lists get credit for duplicate records?
A: There are five main ways of determining which list receives credit and thus payment for duplicate names in a merge/purge of multiple mailing lists. These are as follows:

- *Intentional priority ranking*—ranking by financial, relational, or subjective criteria
- *Random approach*—provides posting "credit" using a technique of first one and then the other list
- *Combination priority and random*—the first few lists are ranked in a priority with all remaining lists receiving random allocation
- *Priority random groupings*—priority groups of lists with random allocation within these groups
- *Matrix data retention*—database construction in which the multiple source and pertinent information can be retained in a file

Q: How do I determine the priority in which the lists should be ranked?
A: There are many ways to determine list priority. Two common ones are:

- *Financial motivation*—such as best net name deal, lowest cost list, etc. In general, the lower the cost of the list or the lower the net name guarantee, the higher the list should be placed in the ranking order

- *Relational motivation*—including business, organizational, and/or personal relationships. These factors could be considered in ranking priority. For example, a list owner who is also the list broker could and probably would choose to place his or her list in a more highly ranked position

Q: What is the difference between a business merge/purge and a consumer merge/purge?
A: There are two primary types of merge/purges:

- Business/institutional

- Consumer/household

To accommodate business marketers, some data service bureaus and list generation companies merely apply business functions to their already created consumer merge/purge software. However, some companies offer a series of distinct programs designed especially for the business-to-business merge/purge.

Business files are more complex and include more fields of information such as company name, job title, department name, etc., all of which are used on the addressing record. On the other hand, consumer files typically only image basic name and address information. Business merge/purge software must be designed to look at the additional fields in order to identify and kill true duplicates and undeliverable records.

Q: What is business chaining and how could it help my mailing?

A: Business chaining is an option your data services provider should offer if you intend on processing a business merge/purge. This process links multiple records within a corporation. Since no records are eliminated, just linked together in a logical manner, you have control as to how many employees per company you wish to mail to.

Q: People advise me that I should test different variables. Can data service providers do this for me? Why should it be done?

A: When working on a direct response marketing program, test different variables to see exactly which ones bring in the highest response rate. Certain lists or list segments will generate higher levels of response. You need to know which ones do. In addition, you need to test various creative elements including envelopes, postage (stamps vs. meter), copy, graphics, etc. You will want to analyze different variables against a control package so you can better target your mailings in the future.

Good data service providers have developed computer software that can split your "test" names and apply different key codes to each list being tested.

Q: Please explain United States Postal Service (USPS) and Canada Post Corporation (CPC) postal presorting. How can it save me money?

A: Postal presorting is the categorizing of data records into different levels of cost-based specifications designed by the USPS and CPC. The basic principle involved is that postal discounts are offered for activities that lower the USPS and CPC mail delivery costs. In general, the more automation-friendly or geographically concentrated your mailing is, the lower your postal costs.

If you take advantage of postal discounts, your mailing services company should provide the Post Office with reports that indicate the quantity of pieces that qualify for each level of discount.

Q: What type of statistics should I get from my merge/purge?

A: Good data services companies will automatically provide you with summary statistics from the output of the merge/purge. This report should tell you the quantity of "inter" and "intra" duplicates for each list included in your merge. It should also provide a listing of the quantity and type of errors for each list. Reports customized to your particular needs should also be made available. An additional report should be made available that shows how many records could not be processed as a result of incorrect postal codes, incomplete addresses, and inaccurate city names, etc.

When you analyze your reports, you should get a good idea of the lists that will work for you. If there is a high duplication rate between your "house" file, if you have one, and other lists, you can be more assured that the people on the outside file are interested in your content and conclude that this list should work well.

Q: How do I get samples to compare different data service providers? Can I get a test done on my file? How much does this cost?

A: This is another good way to tell the difference between service bureaus. Reputable mailing services companies will do tests on a portion of your file at no charge.

Q: What are some differences between USPS and CPC postal systems that your mailing services companies need to be aware of?

A: Canada has a number of unique features to the addressing and postal code systems. Included are:

- The grid system of house and apartment numbering in the western provinces
- The similarity of French language street names (particularly in Quebec and New Brunswick)
- French direction code abbreviations. For example, "O" is the French abbreviation for "W" (West).

It is mandatory that your data service professionals understand these differences during merge/purge.

The Canadian postal coding system is an alphanumeric system, whereas the United States zip code system is numeric only. Both countries are constantly adding, changing, and deleting individual postal codes. Your service bureau must be aware of this and update its software accordingly. In addition, CPC requires mail to be prepared in National Distribution Guide sequence in order to qualify for even the highest level of third-class postage.

Your high-volume mailing services provider should also be able to presort your data and assign Canadian "carrier-walk" or U.S. carrier route codes. If the density of your mailing doesn't warrant postal presorting services, your data services should be able to commingle your mail with other mailings to lower your postal costs.

Q: Since I can't judge merge/purge by price alone, how can I be sure that I am dealing with a good data services company?

A: Choose your computer service bureau the same way you would pick any new employee—interview leading candidates and ask for references. If you like what you hear, you should be more comfortable with your first choice.

Appendix 8

Sample Merge/Purge Report Fields

Merge/Purge Reports

Become familiar with merge/purge reports. It is very important to double-check the output quantity, ensure that the purge file was used correctly, verify the priority of the lists, and review a reasonable sampling of some of the duplicate records.

Explanation of Merge/Purge Reports

Column 1—FILE CODE: Each should have a FILE CODE that distinguishes it for the other files in the merge/purge. This allows separation of the files after the de-duping process to make selections.

Column 2—PRIORITY: Each file in the merge/purge is given a priority. If a duplicate record is found, it will drop from the file with the lower priority.

Column 3—DESCRIPTION: Identifies each input file.

Column 4—INPUT: The input quantity for each file.

Column 5—PRG-DROP: The number of records that drop from each file, resulting from a match to the purge file.

Column 6—MLT-DROP: The number of records that drop because they appear on more than one file (duplicates that occur between files).

Column 7—SNG-DROP: The number of records that
drop because they appear on one file more
than once (duplicates that occur within the
same file).

Column 8—SNG-BUYER: The number of records SAVED
from each file that ONLY appeared on one
input file.

Column 9—MLT-BUYER: The number of records SAVED
from each file that appeared on more than
one input file.

Column 10—OUTPUT: The total number of records saved
from each file.

Column 11—PCT KEPT: The percentage of records that
were saved from each file.

Appendix 9

Presort

The mail presorting process sorts address records into the USPS-required sequence for mail entry into the postal system. These sorting and sequencing processes are based upon mail classification. If done properly, presorting yields substantial postage savings.

Prior to starting the presort process, several pieces of information are needed including:

- Mail class—first, first presort, periodicals, standard A regular, standard A nonprofit, standard B?
- Flat or letter?
- Tray, bag, and/or palletize?
- Size of piece?
- Weight of piece?
- Thickness of piece?
- Automation compatible?
- File list already clean (hygiened)?
- Barcodes required?
- Sort for carrier route discounts—auto/non-auto?
- Process using line of travel?
- Postage method—stamp, meter, or indicia?
- Output—labels, inkjet, or laser?
- Will it be drop-shipped?
- Should it be palletized?
- What should the name and address block look like?

When considering the name and address block keep in mind the OEL Optional Endorsement Line. It appears as the first line in the address block and looks something like this:

**********************CR01*********************

The word "optional" is important. It is required by the USPS to be on mail pieces that are claiming carrier route discounts. If claiming auto/non-auto, five-digit, three-digit, or basic automated rates, the OEL is not required, although it can be since it is useful for mail sorting purposes in the lettershop.

It is important to remember that lettershops needs some way to sort the mail. Either the OEL, pallet, or tray numbers are ideal. During the job planning stages of your mailing, especially when you're creating the name and address block, it's important to consider what sorting information is needed and to assist smooth production.

Appendix 10

Barcode Standards

When using barcodes, be sure that both tabletop and hand-held scanners can read them. Test them on both pieces of equipment. Also, verify the information after it has been read. A common barcode mailing piece identification sequence standard is as follows:

- First 5 digits—job number
- Next 2 digits—cell/lot/version number
- Next 7 digits—unique sequence number

Once the live signoff has been approved, give a sample of the piece to a supervisor. This sample should indicate which barcode should be scanned (if more than one) and show the difference between versions, lots, and cells.

Next, these scanned records should be given on a daily basis to the data processing department. The downloaded quantity should be recorded and checked daily to determine if the number of scanned records seems logical (i.e., you saw a lot of spoilage but only saw 100 recorded in the downloaded file). Then, each week determine if you need to perform the match and reprint the pieces.

Be sure that 100% mailing instructions appear in all tasks, including data processing, addressing, bindery, inserting, and hand work (hand section does the scanning).

Appendix 11

Image Proofing Procedural Standards

Use this checklist to ensure that you have reviewed all possible areas for errors and/or omissions. Watch carefully for:

- Misused words such as "you're" and "your"
- Grammatical errors
- Address positioning errors; cut the form down and put into an actual envelope and do the "tap" test
- Gender match (male name with Mr., female name with Ms.)
- Incorrect initial first name fields
- Default names
- Data table errors

Also, be sure to have a dump of the unconverted records you are using as sign-offs to double-check that data has not changed or been altered during the DP process.

Live Laser Sign-Off Checklist

Endorsement line
- ❏ On all records
- ❏ Only on AUTOCR records
- ❏ Not required

Keyline
- ❏ Customer codes*
- ❏ Sequence no.**
- ❏ Truck/pallet/tray no.

Name and address
- ❏ U/L case
- ❏ Mr. & Mrs.
- ❏ Default title

- ❏ ZIP+4
- ❏ All address lines present
- ❏ Barcode (check it)
- ❏ Shows thru window

Salutation
- ❏ P/U last name/ first name only
- ❏ Default/special salutation
- ❏ Punctuation
- ❏ U/L case
- ❏ Initial only

Body copy/reply

❏ Variable text

❏ Line wraps

❏ Copy on reverse

❏ Form code

❏ Position of copy

❏ $ upgrades calculated OK

❏ Min/max $ $ OK

❏ Rounding correct

Converting samples

❏ Trim OK

❏ Fold OK

❏ Address shows through window

❏ Customer sign-off

❏ Special cells

———

Verify that codes are accurate by counting the number of digits, correct alpha/numeric combination, starting numbers, and comparing to a dump of unconverted record.

Be sure sequence numbers are printed as required. Is it on every record, every 100th, etc.?

Appendix 12

Lettershop Procedures

Success in the lettershop depends on developing good procedures and following them.

Suggested Guidelines

Account managers should prepare complete samples of each version of every job and distribute them appropriately. A good rule of thumb is not to allow any job to begin unless the account manager has provided these samples. All materials should be put in inserting order.

Then, production samples should be pulled several times a day from each producing department and thoroughly examined. Critical things to look for include accurate fold, window position, insertion order, correct material, and version. If there isn't a procedure in place to get these production samples, one should be started. This applies to bindery, addressing, inserting, and saddle stitching.

Account managers should take a few moments several times a day to walk through the area of the plant where their jobs are being processed. Do spot pulls from several machines, look at completed pieces, check the addressing for position, correct information, etc. You may be able to spot a problem before it becomes too serious.

Postal Permits

When working on mailing projects for new customers, be sure to ask if they have their own permits or if they will be using yours. If they have their own, be sure the designated point of entry is suitably located. Sometimes you may have to open a permit for a customer. Either send USPS form 3615 to the customer or fill it out one with the customer's information and submit to the USPS. Each 3615 must be accompanied by a check for $200. The client should advance this fee to you.

These are some examples of indicias. Always have a USPS tech review all new permits before they're used in live production.

```
PRSRT STD
AUTO
U.S. POSTAGE
PAID
BALTIMORE MD
PERMIT 7470
```

```
PRSRT STD
U.S. POSTAGE
PAID
BALTIMORE MD
PERMIT 7470
```

```
FIRST-CLASS MAIL
U.S. POSTAGE
PAID
BALTIMORE MD
PERMIT 7470
```

Appendix 13

An Overs Guide for Specialty Finishing

Please note: The following table should only be used as a guideline for spoilage. Adherence does not necessarily guarantee that a particular project will not be short.

Variables that affect spoilage include the following:

- Temperature and humidity extremes affect equipment, paper, and glue.
- Extreme stock weights—either very heavy or light—are difficult to work with.
- Various varnishes and other paper coatings react differently to different glues and applications.
- Small-quantity projects require a higher percentage of overs compared to large-quantity projects because makeready spoilage is distributed over fewer pieces.
- Multiple code changes and lots increase spoilage requirements. On multiple-code projects, makeready sheets should come from one code. Samples should be provided for each code and be well marked when shipped.

Every project is unique and has its own characteristics. The following guidelines can be used to reduce shortages. However, we do recommend verifying the required overs on every specialty finishing project.

Specialty Finishing Spoilage Guidelines:

Job Description	Example	Required Extra Sheets		
		Makeready	Tune-up	Live Run
Basic folding with glue	4-page folder tipped shut w/fugitive glue	500	500	1%
Difficult folding with glue	Form diecut pocket, 3 rollfolds and double-gate on 100-lb. coated stock	2,000	500	3%
Basic mailer with glue	1 remoist. glue strip, 2 perfs, and fold in half	500	500	3%
Difficult mailer with pattern glue	1-in.-wide glue strip, 2 perfs, 1 time perf, formed pocket with ½-in. short rollfolds on 50-lb. stock	2,000	500	10%
High-level custom-designed	Hot-melt U-shaped glue, time cutting, 2nd remoist. glue strip, pocket-glue to create BRC inside zipper perf	5,000	1,000	10%
Inkjet imaging	Four 8-line address	500	100	1%

Appendix 14

Drop Ship Logistics

Make sure your drop ship logistics are handled properly.
Your direct mail services provider should have a completely
developed drop shipping procedure that requires the
account managers to do the following:

• Provide "ready dates," "entry dates," and "in-home
dates." The *ready date* is the day the mail is ready to leave
the facility. The *entry date* is the day the mail is to be
entered into BMCs, SCFs, and DDUs. The *in-home dates*
are the days that the mail pieces should be delivered to
the recipient.

• Receive and review a transportation plan from the logistics department. This document must show all trailers and
stops. If necessary, indicate any changes and circulate it
to the appropriate people. Once the plan is approved, the
account manager will receive the final transportation plan
and "plant load" sheets.

• Once mail is entered into the BMC/SCF/DDU, the
account manager should receive documentation with the
trailer number, destination, city, state, delivery date,
date/time mail was accepted, and person who accepted
the mail. This information can be passed on to the client
on a regular basis, if requested.

Weight Sheets

Weight sheets should be created as processed mail is
loaded onto drop ship transportation or USPS transportation. The account manager should receive copies of these
weight sheets every morning and double-check the destinations and weights for assurance that the job is proceeding
as planned.

Appendix 15

Managing Client Samples

Samples are required on most jobs. Check with your customer prior to creating your job order ticket to see what kind of samples they want—"live" or "Sample A" samples. Ask if they require samples of the laser and personalization only or samples of the entire package. How many samples do they want and at what production stage do they want them to be pulled from? Is there a special sample lot to produce samples from?

If "Sample A" sample packages are required, be sure to discuss this with your data center, include it in a production flowchart, and detail client-specific needs on the job order. If live records are required for the samples, again be sure to discuss with the data center and include detailed instructions on the order. Usually it's best to run all samples at the beginning of the job or at the beginning of each code or cell.

Sample requirements should be detailed on the job order form for the mail plant. Face-to-face discussions between account managers and plant supervisors are encouraged if the instructions are either complex or new. Actual trimmed and assembled pre-production sample packages are the best way to let everyone know what your customers expect.

Appendix 16

Account Management Materials Handling Tips

Incoming Material

Get receiving tickets and samples of all incoming material. "Preflight" the job once all components are in. Included in this process is double-checking that all materials are the correct size and color, folds can be positioned properly, etc. Don't assume that since the correct sample is attached to the receipt, that the receipt reflects the correct inventory identification number. This can be very costly and time-consuming.

Receiving

Let your suppliers know your shipping hours, maximum pallet size, and any special requirements. For example, if you don't accept pallets that are stacked higher than 50 in. (1.27 m) or are unwrapped, say so.

If your continuous forms must be delivered upright, with one or two to a skid, let your suppliers know. If accepting rolls stacked poker chip style (laying down flat on their sides) causes production problems, don't accept them delivered this way.

Shipping/Outbound Material

All shipped material should be accompanied by a properly completed bill of lading (delivery ticket). Make sure the warehouse/logistics departments get a copy and that it includes:

- Client name, job name, and number
- Description of each piece

- Number of items including boxes, skids, trays, and overall quantity
- Exact delivery address with contact name and phone number
- Expected ship date and arrival date

In addition, a "pull ticket" should be created and sent to the warehouse for printing. This "pull ticket" notifies the warehouse personnel that they should take the material out of warehouse and stage it for shipping.

If you are shipping completed mail that mails from somewhere other than your facility, include a weight sticker with each pallet. Although the warehouse staff should do this task, the account manager still should make sure that each pallet is accounted for as it is placed on the outbound truck. Also, at this point account managers should perform an inventory on the excess material to check quantities. Be sure that material being returned makes sense after considering what was received and produced.

Excess or Leftover Material

Account managers should try to obtain excess material disposition instructions from customers prior to distributing the order. A reasonable policy is to destroy excess materials after 30 days unless specific instructions for disposition were received prior to beginning work on the job.

However, don't destroy any materials unless an actual sample of the piece is sent to the warehouse or some other department in charge of keeping production records. This means that when the warehouse is advised to destroy or recycle material, they will require not only written instructions and pull tickets, but they will also require an actual sample of the material to be destroyed. If there is similar material in house, characteristics that differentiate between the pieces should be clearly marked or indicated so that warehouse personnel will not have difficulty identifying the correct material.

Warehouse/logistics employees should participate in this procedure by saving a sample from each pallet being destroyed. Then, they can compare the sample piece provided, write a destroy date on each extracted piece, and return the dated pieces to the account managers once all material has been removed.

Billing Job Jacket

Certain documents should be kept in job jackets. These files can and will be audited by the USPS for accuracy. Keeping these specific documents will support mailing claims, if they occur. Each jacket must contain:

- Customer signed quote, job confirmation receipt, or purchase order
- Completed copy of internal job order
- Mailing statements (3602s, 3606s)
- Job quantity summary sheets by postal tier (from postal software)
- Discrepancy/shortage sheet (if needed)
- Any revised order or information
- Sample boards
- Ten or more samples verified by USPS
- Production history report from mail software
- Job activity report from mail software
- ICH facing slips (if used)
- Drop ship/plant load sheet
- Disposition (excess material) sheet
- Error sheet (if needed)

- Transportation charges (each client should have established transportation rates and should be billed along with production and DP charges)
- Postage billing codes

When the job jacket comes from the accounting department, make sure that postage information has been detailed for you. Sample codes are as follows:

- P1—Permit 7470
- P2—Metered postage
- P3—Stamps
- P4—Less customer advance
- P6—Less escrow
- P7—Return to escrow
- P8—Verification fees
- P9—Postage refund

Be sure to check the postage figures carefully and indicate what to do with excess postage—pay down the invoice, put into escrow, or send a refund check.

Appendix 17

Fulfillment

Once responses to a direct mail program have been captured, all requests must be fulfilled. Some direct mail services companies offer fulfillment services to their clients. If you outsource your fulfillment requirements and you're interested in a single-source relationship with your mailer, make sure there's a good match between your needs and their fulfillment capabilities.

First, determine what type of fulfillment services you will need. Here are the three basic categories:

- *Information fulfillment*—collateral materials, tele-responses, more direct mail pieces, sales visits, etc.
- *Complementary product fulfillment*—supplying a product without any required payment
- *Paid product fulfillment*—supplying a product with a required payment

The process of fulfillment is a uniquely manual procedure that usually requires more attention and procedures than may appear at first glance. For example, fulfilling a dozen requests within an office environment is a simple, albeit time-consuming task. Fulfilling hundreds or thousands of requests is a logistics process few nonprofessionals are capable of completing without crossing many quality, insurance, and administrative hurdles.

If a product is being fulfilled, make sure that your fulfillment services provider has a clear understanding of your needs as well as how communication (verbal and digital) flows between client and vendor. An appropriate inventory tracking and control system is also necessary.

The timeliness of fulfilling requests is the basis by which organizations are measured. The timing will be evaluated based upon the expectations set within the original communication. Be sure if your original communication states "allow two weeks for delivery" that your processing, on average, will get it to them in one week.

Appendix 18

Typical Grain Direction on Cut-Sheet Laser Printers

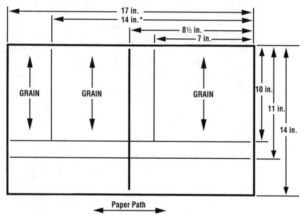

*Above 14 in. must be landscape, therefore must be 10 in. in width.

Appendix 19

Common Folding Diagrams

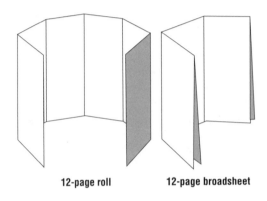

12-page roll   12-page broadsheet

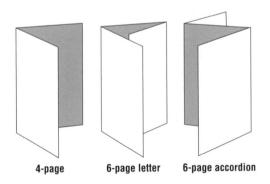

4-page   6-page letter   6-page accordion

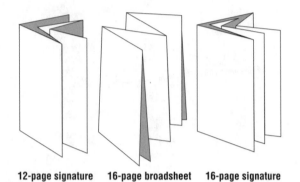

12-page signature **16-page broadsheet** **16-page signature**

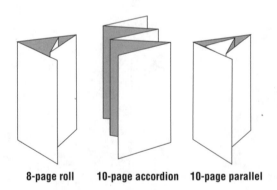

8-page roll **10-page accordion** **10-page parallel**

Direct Mail Pal

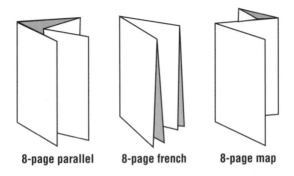

8-page parallel   **8-page french**   **8-page map**

GLOSSARIES

Glossary 1—Data Terms

Active subscriber—A person or organization that has committed to receive regular delivery of magazines, books, other goods, or services for a time period still in effect.

Address accuracy—The level of matches that a database attains when compared to a national address database. The accuracy of a mailing list (over 10,000 records) is required to be at least 95% accurate to qualify for best postal rates.

Address correction—The process of correcting addresses to match a national address database. This step is taken when a list does meet the 95% criteria (most lists require correction).

Address correction requested—An endorsement that authorizes the USPS (United States Postal Service) or CPC (Canada Post Corporation) a fee to provide the new address, when known, of a person no longer at the address on the mailing piece.

ASCII (American Standard Code for Information Interchange)—A standard eight-bit data configuration in which seven bits are used to store data characters and, typically, the eighth bit is a parity bit.

Assigned mailing date(s)—The date(s) on which the list owner and the list user have agreed for the list user to mail a specific list.

Block—A specified quantity of logical records stored together between inter-record gaps, constituting a physical record.

Blocking factor—A statement of the number of logical records combined into one physical record or block on a storage medium, usually magnetic tape, between inter-record gaps.

BPI (bytes per inch)—The number of characters stored in an inch of magnetic tape. Commonly used densities are 800, 1,600, and 6,250.

Bulk mail center (BMC)—A large U.S. postal facility (currently there are 29 of them) that process and distribute mail to various SCFs.

Business list—Any list of individuals or companies based upon a business-associated interest, inquiry, membership, subscription, or purchase.

Buyer—One who has bought merchandise, books, records, information, or services. Unless another modifying word or two is used, it is assumed that a buyer has paid for all merchandise to date.

Buzzing—The process by which a computer program continuously selects various components within a name and address, and compares them to similar components in another record, thereby checking thousands of possibilities to locate a duplicate.

Carrier route presort (USPS)—Mail that identifies the carrier route number for mail delivery. Mailers who sort down to carrier route can mail at a carrier route discount rate.

Cartridge (data cartridge)—A commonly used, transportable storage device for data coming from different computer systems. Cartridges are available in many *incompatible* shapes and sizes.

Cash buyer—A buyer who encloses payment with the order.

Catalog request (paid/unpaid)—A person who sends for a catalog, often a prospective buyer. The catalog may be free, have a nominal charge for postage and handling, or available only at a substantial cost.

Cathode-ray tube display (CRT display)—(1) A device that presents data in a visual form by means of controlled electron beams. (2) The data display produced by the device as in (1).

Charge buyer—One who has ordered a product or service and paid for it after receipt of the product or service.

Cheshire label—Specially prepared paper on which names and addresses are printed before being mechanically affixed to a mailing piece, one at a time with permanent glue.

Cluster selection—A selection routine based upon taking a group of names in series, skipping a group, taking another group, etc. For example, a cluster selection on an *Nth* name basis might be the first 10 out of every 100 or the first 125 out of 175, etc.; a cluster selection using limited postal code might be the first 200 names in each of the specified postal codes, etc.

Compiled list—Names and addresses derived from directories, newspapers, public records, tradeshow registrations, etc., that identify groups of people via a common link.

Consumer list—A list of names (usually at-home address) of people who have purchased merchandise, subscriptions, services, etc., from mail, Internet, radio, or TV solicitations.

Conversion—See *reformatting*.

Cross section—A group of names and addresses selected from a mailing list in such a way as to be representative of the entire list.

Database (list)—A number of lists, presumably with common interest, merged into one master list with duplicates eliminated.

Date control character (DCC)—The code applied to a presorted record that denotes the period of time for which a sortation is valid. As the configuration of ZIP and postal codes change on a regular basis, each postal database is refreshed frequently, which ensures that each mail piece bears current information and can be delivered accurately.

Decoy—See *salting and seed.*

Demographics—Socioeconomic characteristics pertaining to a geographic unit (county, city, postal code, group of households, etc.).

Density (storage density)—A measure of the number of characters stored in a specified amount of space. For example, the number of characters per inch of magnetic tape (bytes per inch.)

Destination delivery unit (DDU)—A local U.S. post office. DDUs tier up to SCFs.

Disk (magnetic diskette, floppy diskette)—A commonly used, transportable storage device for small amounts of data coming from a PC.

DMA Mail Order Action Line (MOAL)—A service provided by the Direct Marketing Association to assist consumers who have encountered problems while shopping by mail which they have not been able to resolve through direct contact with the mailer.

DMA Mail Preference Service (MPS)—A service provided by the Direct Marketing Association that enables individuals to have their names and addresses removed from mailing lists. These names are made available to both members and nonmembers of the association. For individuals who specify that they would like to receive more mail, special instructions for this purpose are forwarded.

Donor list—A list of people and organizations that have given money to one or more charitable organizations.

Dump—Printed display of the contents of a data file, typically a magnetic tape or a portion of that data file, for purposes of review of the data.

Duplicate (dupe)—Two or more name and address records that are found to be equal under the list user's basis of comparison (match code, mathematical formula, etc.). Essentially, it is a record that matches another record. There are different kinds of duplicates. Personal dupes are the same person at the same address. Household dupes are different people at the same address.

Duplicate elimination—See *merge/purge*.

EBCDC (Extended Binary Coded Decimal Interchange Code)—This is an eight-bit configuration used to represent up to 256 separate characters (alpha, numeric, and special characters). EBCDIC uses the eighth bit as an information bit, which differs from ASCII, which uses one of the eight for parity.

Editing Rules—Specific rules used in preparing name and address records in order to treat all elements the same way at all times. Although most companies use some editing rules in common, few conform in all respects. Therefore, knowledge of specific editing rules for each list is important to the user.

Escalation—The number of names ordered after a test. (See also *pyramiding*.)

Expire—A subscriber who has let a subscription run out without renewing it.

Field—A segment of a record that contains specific information. In a database, fields should contain the same information for each record. For example, all name fields should contain a name, all postal code fields should contain a postal code, etc.

Fielding—Technique by which the name and address of a record are divided into specific components.

File—A collection of records on a single storage device.

File layout—A way of laying out or formatting list information in a computer file that puts every piece of data in a specific position relative to every other piece of data and limits the amount of space assigned to that data. If any data is missing from an individual record or if its assigned space is not used completely, that space is not filled. Every record has the same space and the same length. Any data exceeding its assigned space limitation must be abbreviated, contracted, or truncated. (See also *record layout*.)

Forward sortation area (FSA)—(Canada only) A three-character code indicating a Canada Post Corporation distribution area. It is the first three characters of the six-character postal code. In urban areas, it describes an area roughly the size of 25 letter carrier routes.

Free standing insert—A promotional piece loosely inserted or nested in a newspaper or magazine.

Frequency—The number of times an individual has ordered within a specific period of time. (See also *recency*.)

House list (house file)—Any list of names owned by a company as a result of inquiry, buyer action, or specific targeting (usually with research).

Inter-list duplicate—Duplication of name and address records between two or more lists.

Intra-list duplicate—Duplication of name and address records within a given list.

Key code—Numbers or letters appended to a record that appear on a label, letter, reply, etc., which indicate a source of that name or segmentation for a mailing. This data is used for tracking and evaluation purposes.

Letter carrier presort (LCP)—Sequencing Canadian addresses by postal walk in order to obtain the highest possible postal discount when mailing third class.

Letter mail—CPC term for first-class mail.

Lettershop—A manufacturing facility (internal or external) that prepares mail for delivery to the USPS (United States Postal Service) or CPC (Canada Post Corporation).

List broker—A specialist who makes all necessary arrangements for one company to use the list(s) of other company(s). A broker's services may include most or all of the following: research, selection, recommendation, and subsequent evaluation.

List cleaning—The process of correcting and/or removing a name and address from a mailing list because it is no longer correct. Addresses may be corrected as a result of information furnished by the Postal Service or the individual. (See also *address correction requested*.) Removal may be the result of the return of a mailing piece by the Postal Service. (See also *return postage guaranteed*.)

Local delivery unit (LDU)—The last three characters of a Canadian postal code that denote a very small and easily defined section within an area described by the FSA. These characters can specify one side of a city block, an apartment building, an office building, or a large firm or organization that does considerable business with the CPC. They can also denote a service from a post office or postal station.

Magnetic tape (mag tape)—A storage device for electronically recording and reproducing defined bits of data.

Merge—To combine multiple lists into a single list, all of which have the same file layout.

Merge/purge (duplicate elimination)—Combining two or more lists on a computer for the purpose of eliminating duplicate names and identifying multiple-buyers among the lists being used. Reports are then issued indicating, by list, the number of unique names, inter-file duplicates, assigned multi-buyers, and other pertinent information.

Net name arrangement—An agreement between list owner and list user in which the list owner agrees to accept adjusted payment for less than the total names shipped. Such arrangements can be for a percentage of names shipped or names actually mailed (whichever is greater), or for only those names actually mailed (without a percentage limitation). They can provide for a running charge or not. (See *running charge*.)

Nine-digit ZIP code (ZIP+4)—Within the United States, this provides for encoding each block face, each post office box, and each volume mail recipient with a unique nine-digit number.

Nixie—A mailing piece returned to a mailer (under proper authorization) by the Postal Service because of an incorrect or undeliverable name and address.

Nth name selection—A fractional unit that is repeated in sampling mailing list. For example, in an "every tenth" sample, you would select the 1st, 11th, 21st, 31st, etc. records or the 2nd, 12th, 22nd, 32nd, etc. records. Fractional *N*ths can also be processed.

Output—(1) The final results after a computer has processed data. (2) Information that has been transferred from the internal storage of a computer to external storage. (3) The process of transferring data from internal to external storage—e.g., mag tape, hard copy printout, diskette, inkjet, etc. The client should always provide a document or sample of the mail piece indicating which fields in a given record are to be used when personalizing the mail piece.

Overlay—The process by which information is added to a main or master file to enable a more specialized selection.

Packed decimal—A means of data representation in which two numeric digits may be stored in a single eight-bit byte, thus increasing processing speed and storage capacity while minimizing record length in circumstances where neither alphabetic nor special characters need to be used.

Patterning—Technique that uses a series of words, word types, addresses, and address types to segment, standardize, and identify similarities and differences in the names and addresses of a file.

Penetration—Relationship of the number of individuals or families on a particular list (in total, by province, postal code, SIC code, etc.), compared to the total reachable population in the same area.

Point scoring—A flexible parameter set to determine the level in which a "possible duplicate" is identified as a "definite duplicate."

Postal code (Canada)—A group of six characters used by Canada Post Corporation to designate specific post offices, stations, branches, buildings, or large companies. In urban areas, the LDU in conjunction with the FSA contain enough information to determine the destination of a letter right down to one side of a city street between intersections, and sometimes even further.

Pressure-sensitive label—A label that can be removed from its backing and reaffixed to another surface, such as an order form.

Printout—A hard copy display of information or data.

Psychographics—Characteristics or qualities used to denote the lifestyle(s) or attitude(s) of customers or prospective customers.

Purge—To remove records from a list, typically duplicate records.

Pyramiding—A method of testing mailing lists, starting with a small quantity and, based on positive indications, following with larger and larger quantities of the balance of the list until the entire list is finally mailed.

Recency—The latest purchase or other activity recorded for an individual or company on a specific customer list. (See also *frequency*.)

Record—A collection of related data or words treated as one unit.

Record layout—A written, field-by-field description of the data contained in a record, typically describing each field as to its length, beginning and ending positions, name, editing characteristics and data format (i.e., character, hex packed, etc.). (See also *file layout*.)

Reformatting—Changing a magnetic tape format from one arrangement to another more usable one. Also referred to as list or tape conversion.

Rented list—Lists that are rented by the organization performing the mailing.

Return date—The date specified on a list rental order on which the material is required by the mailers so that the mailing can get out on time.

Return postage guaranteed—An endorsement printed on the address face of envelopes or other mailing pieces if the mailer wishes the Postal Service to return undeliverable standard (U.S.)/third-class bulk (Canada) mail. A charge will be made for each piece returned (see also *list cleaning*).

Running charge—The price charged by a list owner for names run or passed, but not used, by a specific mailer. When such a charge is made, it usually covers extra processing costs. However, some list owners set the price without regard to actual cost.

Salting—Deliberate placing of decoy or dummy names in a list to trace list usage and delivery. (See also *decoy and seed.*)

Sample package (mailing piece)—An example of the package to be mailed by the list user to a particular list. Such a mailing piece is submitted to the list owner for approval prior to commitment for one-time use of that list. Although a sample package may, due to time pressure, differ slightly from the actual package used, the list user agreement usually requires the user to reveal any material differences when submitting the sample package.

Scratch—The process by which a physical reel of magnetic tape that contains a data file is made available for reuse when there is no longer any need to retain the data file. In general, this process involves obtaining authorization (from the responsible account service person) to scratch, removing physical external labels from the reel, placing a write ring in the physical reel, and updating tape library records.

Section center facility (SCF)—A U.S. postal facility that is positioned between DDUs and BMCs.

Seed—A name especially inserted into a mailing list for verification of list usage. It has unique characteristics, such as an order number or a unique spelling, that indicates order for which it was used. (See also *decoy and salting*.)

Select—To choose a group of records from a database based on a given criteria.

SIC (Standard Industrial Classification)—Classification of business, as defined by the Canadian and U.S. governments.

Sort—A processing function that arranges a file in a specified sequence.

Source code—Unique alphabetical and/or numeric identification for distinguishing one list or media source from another. (See also *key code*.)

Split test—Two or more samples from the same list, selected by the same criteria (such as an A/B split) used for testing different packages, offers, mail dates, or any other part of the mailing.

Suppress (suppression)—To eliminate certain records based on a given criteria.

Tape density—The number of bits of information that can be included in each inch of a specific magnetic tape (e.g., 556, 800, or 1,600).

Tape dump—A printout of data on a magnetic tape for checking correctness, readability, consistency, etc.

Tape layout—A written, field-by-field description of the data contained in a record, typically describing each field as to its length, beginning and ending positions, name, editing characteristics, and data format (i.e., character, hex, packed, etc.).

Test panel—A term used to identify each of the parts or samples in a split test.

Title—A designation before (prefix) or after (suffix) a name that more accurately identifies an individual. Prefixes include Mr., Mrs., Ms., Dr., Sister, etc. Suffixes include MD, Jr., PhD, President, Sales Manager, etc.

Truncate—To drop characters at the end of a data field because the field being converted or keyed in is too long to fit in the record position in which it must be stored.

Universe count—The total number on a list available within a particular selection, taking no account of prior usage.

Update—Adding recent transactions and current information to the master (main) list to reflect the current status of each record on the list.

Upper/lower conversion—Converting a database, commonly all in capital letters, to uppercase and lowercase letters. (Note: Upper/lower conversion is not 100% accurate. For example, some names such as MacArthur may result in Macarthur.)

Variable field—A way of laying out or formatting list information that assigns a specific sequence to the data, but does not assign it specific positions. While this method conserves space on magnetic tape and adds flexibility for the end user, it generally is a more difficult format for programmers.

ZIP codes—A group of five digits used by the U.S. Postal Service to designate specific post offices, stations, branches, buildings, or large companies.

Glossary 2—Lettershop Terms

Bindery—Conversion of printed sheet into finished product.

Cheshire label—An address label that is approximately 1 in. (25 mm) deep and 3 in. (76 mm) wide. Often used for catalogs and books. For example, *TV Guide* uses Cheshire labels.

Closed leading edge—The leading edge of a piece going into an envelope should be folded.

Digitize—A logo, signature, or any graphic that can be digitized and then laser-imaged onto a page. This allows for different signatures or logos to be used in the same mailing yet retain the density of the mailing to receive maximum postal discounts.

Friction feeder—An add-on piece of equipment used to facilitate the insertion of a piece with an open leading edge, such as an accordion-folded piece.

Indicia (permit)—The preprinted block in the upper right-hand corner of an address area, which signifies that a mailing has been paid for. Permits are available for standard, first, and catalog classes.

Inkjet imaging—A manner of addressing a mail piece (self-mailer, envelope, catalog, etc.). The address area of the mail piece is run under a head that sprays fine "jets" of ink to generate an address. Inkjet imaging is usually used to personalize addresses and possibly account numbers.

Laser—A means of personalizing an entire page of information. Typically used for more involved personalization and letter type direct mail for a slicker look. More personalized look equates to a higher cost. Used quite often for financial and high-end promotion.

Laser, continuous—Laser imaging that is performed in a continuous format, either fan-folded or on rolls. Typically used for larger runs since setup costs are high.

Laser, cut-sheet—Laser imaging that is performed on single sheets. Sheet sizes can be from 8½×11 in. (216×279 mm) to 14×17 in. (356×432 mm). Odd sizes and grain direction should be discussed prior to quoting.

Mail preparation (sort, bag, and bundle)—The process of preparing mail in order to obtain second- or third-class postage rates.

Meter—A means of affixing postage to an envelope. Meters are set to affix a certain amount of postage to an envelope and can be used for first class, standard mail, and parcels. Meter money is required prior to mail production.

Oversize—A term for standard mail pieces that have dimensions exceeding standard sizes. Oversize pieces involve higher postal costs and usually cost more to produce.

INDEX

A

B

C

D

T

U

V

W

Z

About the Authors

T.J. Tedesco is the president of Grow Sales, Inc., a consulting company serving the graphic arts industry. He helps graphic arts companies win more profitable business by winning top-of-mind positioning. Grow Sales, Inc., offers the following services: marketing management, customer nurture programs, sales and management coaching, seminars, public speaking, strategic marketing plans, ghostwritten trade articles, and public relations work.

Tedesco has a B.A. in English from Grinnell College and an MBA in Marketing & Finance from Northeastern University, where he was class valedictorian. He is a well-known speaker in the graphic arts industry and is a regular columnist for *High Volume Printing* and *The Binding Edge*. In addition, he has had articles published in dozens of other well-known graphic arts publications.

Prior to launching his consulting business, Tedesco was the director of marketing for a large graphic arts company and a product manager for a consumer products company. He also has sold graphic arts machinery, printing, and binding services. He started his career in finance with a Fortune 100 company.

Tedesco is the author of *Binding, Finishing & Mailing: The Final Word* (GATFPress, 1999) and co-author of *Win Top-of-Mind Positioning* (GATFPress, 2000). He lives in Rockville, Maryland, and can be reached at (301) 294-9900 or tj@growsales.com. His company's website is www.growsales.com.

Ken Boone began in the marketing business as a child in Dundalk, Maryland, by delivering circulars for Advanced Distribution of Maryland. He rejoined the company as a salesman after graduating from Shepherd College in Shepherdstown, West Virginia, in 1976. After three years, he launched his own company, Direct Marketing Associates, with very limited capital. Under Boone's leadership and rapid growth ambitions, twenty years later, DMA employed more than 500 people. In 1999, he sold DMA to Harte-Hanks, Inc., a NYSE-traded company.

Boone is a well-known speaker and author in the direct mail industry. He has been a regular contributor to publications such as *DM News* and *Advents*. Boone splits his time between Florida and Maryland and can be reached at KenBoone0213@aol.com.

Terry Woods is a well-respected direct mail expert, former co-principal of Direct Marketing Associates, Inc., and former president of Harte-Hanks Baltimore. He is a native of Baltimore, Maryland, and graduated from Towson State University where he earned a B.S. degree in Business with concentrations in Finance and Labor Relations.

Woods joined Direct Marketing Associates Inc. in 1982. In 1986 he became a co-principal of DMA and was elevated to vice president. He held that position until May 1999 when DMA was purchased by Harte-Hanks, Inc. He is a regular contributor to publications such as *DM News* and *Advents*.

Woods lives in Timonium, Maryland, and can be reached at 410-308-9002 or terrywoods4@comcast.net.

John Leonard is vice president, sales and marketing for SMR/Tytrek, located in Toronto, Canada. Leonard has a degree in general advertising and started his career with a direct marketing company owned by Grey Advertising. When this company was sold to SMR, he shifted his attention to sales and customer service.

In 1997 SMR merged with the oldest specialty finishing organization in Canada, Tytrek Graphic Finishers. Today, SMR/Tytrek is one of Canada's premier specialty mailing services companies, offering a diverse array of binding, finishing, and mailing services. There Leonard was promoted to vice president, sales and marketing. In addition, he is part-time faculty member at Mohawk College.

Leonard can be reached at 416-461-9271 or jleonard@smrtytrek.com

About GATF

The Graphic Arts Technical Foundation is a nonprofit, scientific, technical, and educational organization dedicated to the advancement of the graphic communications industries worldwide. Its mission is to serve the field as the leading resource for technical information and services through research and education. GATF partners with the Printing Industries of America (PIA), the world's largest printing industry trade association.

For 78 years the Foundation has developed leading edge technologies and practices for printing. GATF's staff of researchers, educators, and technical specialists partner with nearly 14,000 corporate members in over 80 countries to help them maintain their competitive edge by increasing productivity, print quality, process control, and environmental compliance, and by implementing new techniques and technologies. Through conferences, satellite symposia, workshops, consulting, technical support, laboratory services, and publications, GATF strives to advance a global graphic communications community.

The GATFPress publishes books on nearly every aspect of the field; learning modules (step-by-step instruction booklets); audiovisuals (CD-ROMs and videocassettes); and research and technology reports. It also publishes *GATFWorld,* a bimonthly magazine of technical articles, industry news, and reviews of specific products.

For more detailed information on GATF products and services, please visit *www.gain.net,* or write to 200 Deer Run Road, Sewickley, PA 15143-2600 (phone: 412/741-6860).

GRAPHIC ARTS TECHNICAL FOUNDATION

About PIA

In operation since 1887 and headquartered in Alexandria, Virginia, Printing Industries of America, Inc. (PIA), is the world's largest graphic arts trade association representing an industry with more than 1 million employees and $156 billion in sales annually. PIA promotes the interests of more than 14,000 member companies. Companies become members in PIA by joining one of 30 regional affiliate organizations throughout the United States or by joining the Canadian Printing Industries Association. International companies outside North America may join PIA directly. Printing Industries of America, Inc. is in the business of promoting programs, services, and an environment that helps its members operate profitably. Many of PIA's members are commercial printers, allied graphic arts firms such as electronic imaging companies, equipment manufacturers, and suppliers.

PIA has developed several special industry groups to meet the unique needs of specific market segments. Each special industry group provides members with current information on their specific market and helps members stay ahead of the competition. PIA's special industry groups are the Web Offset Association (WOA), Web Printing Association (WPA), Graphic Arts Marketing Information Service (GAMIS), Label Printing Industries of America (LPIA), and Binding Industries of America International (BIA).

For more information on PIA products and services, please visit *www.gain.net* or write to 100 Daingerfield Road, Alexandria, VA 22314 (phone: 703/519-8100).

PRINTING INDUSTRIES of AMERICA

GATF*Press:* Selected Titles

The Basics of Print Production. Hardesty, Mary

Binding, Finishing, and Mailing: The Final Word. Tedesco, T.J.

Customer Service in the Printing Industry. Colbary, Richard E.

Flexography Primer. Crouch, J. Page

The GATF Encyclopedia of Graphic Communications.
Romano, Frank J. & Richard M. Romano

The GATF Guide to Desktop Publishing. Hinderliter, Hal

Glossary of Graphic Communications. Groff, Pamela J.

Gravure Primer. Kasunich, Cheryl L.

Handbook of Graphic Arts Equations. Breede, Manfred

Lithography Primer. Wilson, Daniel G.

*Nine Steps to Effective and Efficient Color Press OKs
for Offset Printing.* Biegert, Diane J.

On-Demand and Digital Printing Primer. Fenton, Howard M.

Paper Buying Primer. Wilson, Lawrence A.

Professional Print Buying. Green, Phil

Real-Time Marketing: New Rules for the New Media.
Morris-Lee, James

Screen Printing Primer. Ingram, Samuel T.

Understanding Graphic Communication: Selected Readings.
Levenson, Harvey Robert.

*The Very Last Designer's Guide to Digital, On-Demand, and
Variable-Data Color Printing.* Clark, David & Frank J. Romano

*Win Top-of-Mind Positioning: Graphic Arts Sales & Marketing
Excellence.* Tedesco, T.J., Mike Stevens, & Henry Mortimer

Colophon

Direct Mail Pal was edited, designed, and printed at the Graphic Arts Technical Foundation, headquartered in Sewickley, Pennsylvania. The text was created by the author using Microsoft Word, then edited at GATF and imported into QuarkXPress 4.0 on an Apple Macintosh G4. The primary fonts used for the interior of the book are Gill Sans and Eurostile Condensed. Pages for author approval were proofed on a Xerox Regal color copier with Splash RIP.

Once the editorial/page layout process was completed, the images were transmitted to GATF's Robert Howard Center for Imaging Excellence, where all images were adjusted for the printing parameters of GATF's in-house printing department and proofed.

After the book was preflighted using a Apple Macintosh G4, Heidelberg's Prinergy production system was used to impose the pages, and then the book was output to a Creo Trendsetter 3244 platesetter. The interior of the book was printed on GATF's 26×40-in., four-color Heidelberg Speedmaster Model 102-4P sheetfed perfecting press, and the cover was printed two-up on GATF's 20×28-in., six-color Komori Lithrone 28 sheetfed press with tower coater. Finally, the book was sent to a trade bindery for perfect binding.